SOPHOCLES

WORLD DRAMATISTS

In the same series:

WORLD DRAMATISTS

SOPHOCLES

SIEGFRIED MELCHINGER

Translated by David A. Scrase

WITH HALFTONE ILLUSTRATIONS

FREDERICK UNGAR PUBLISHING CO.

NEW YORK

PA
4417
M 4513

Translated from the German Sophokles
Published by arrangement with Friedrich Verlag,
Velber, Germany

Copyright © 1974 by Frederick Ungar Publishing Co., Inc.
Printed in the United States of America
Library of Congress Catalog Card Number: 72-79931
Designed by Edith Fowler
ISBN: 0-8044-2617-1 (cloth)

65518

CONTENTS

CHRONOLOGY

court of appeals, is deprived of its power. Cimon is exiled.

461   Ephialtes is assassinated, and Pericles becomes the leading statesman in Athens.

462–32   The philosopher Anaxagoras teaches in Athens; among his pupils are Pericles and Euripides.

458   Aeschylus' *Oresteia* is performed in Athens. Aeschylus emigrates to Sicily.

456   Aeschylus dies in Sicily.

455   Euripides' *The Peliades*, his first play to be performed at the dionysian dramatic festival, wins third prize.

450–447 (?)   Sophocles' *Ajax* is performed in Athens.

443   Sophocles becomes treasurer of the Attic Naval League.

442   Sophocles' *Antigone* is performed at the dionysian theater.

441   Euripides emerges for the first time as victor at the dionysian dramatic festival with a play that is not known to us.

440 (?)   Sophocles' *The Women of Trachis* is performed in Athens.

438   Euripides' *Alcestis* is performed for the first time in Athens. The Parthenon is dedicated to Pallas Athena.

437   Construction of the Propylaea, on the Acropolis, begins.

431   Euripides' *Medea* is performed in Athens. The Peloponnesian War breaks out between Athens and Sparta.

430 (?)   Euripides' *Children of Heracles* is performed in Athens.

430–29   The plague rages in Athens.

429   Sophocles' *Oedipus the King* is performed at the dionysian theater. Pericles dies of the plague. Nicias becomes the

leader of the party of the aristocrats, and Cleon the leader of the democrats.

ca. 428   Euripides' *Hippolytus* is performed in Athens.

427   Aristophanes achieves his first victory at the dionysian dramatic festival. The Spartan troops invade Attica. A punitive expedition against Mytilene is carried out. Plato is born.

425 (?)   Euripides' *Hecuba* is performed. Aristophanes' *Acharnians* is performed at the lenaean festival.

421   A peace treaty is signed between Sparta and Athens, known as the Peace of Nicias, who represented Athens. Aristophanes' *The Peace* is performed while the negotiations go on. The stone structure for the theater and the Erechtheum, on the Acropolis, are started.

ca. 421   Euripides' *Heracles* is performed in Athens. His *Cyclops* is performed. *The Suppliant Women* is written.

420   Alcibiades becomes an influential force in Athenian politics.

418   Renewed fighting breaks out between Athens and Sparta.

416   The Athenians attack Melos and massacre the population.

415   Euripides' *The Trojan Women* is performed in Athens.

415–13   The Athenians organize an expedition against Sicily, which ends in disaster for the Athenians. Alcibiades is ostracized by the Athenians and goes over to the enemy side.

ca. 414   Euripides' *Iphigenia in Tauris* is performed.

413	Euripides' *Ion* is performed in Athens. Spartans lay siege to Decelea and the war engulfs Attica. Archelaus comes to the throne of Macedonia. A probouleutic council is established in Athens.
ca. 413	Euripides' *Electra* is performed.
ca. 413	Sophocles' *Electra* is performed at the dionysian theater.
412	Euripides' *Helen* is performed in Athens. Many of Athens's allies revolt against her. Sparta forms an alliance with Persia.
411	Aristophanes' *The Thesmophoriazusae* is performed in Athens. Revolution breaks out in Athens and democracy is abolished. Alcibiades is recalled to Athens.
410	Euripides' *The Phoenician Maidens* is performed in Athens. Democracy is restored in Athens. Alcibiades becomes chief admiral of the navy.
409	Sophocles' *Philoctetes* is performed at the dionysian theater.
408	Euripides' *Orestes* is performed.
407	Euripides emigrates to Pella in Macedonia. Alcibiades is deposed.
406	Euripides dies in Pella.
405	Sophocles dies in Athens. Euripides' *Iphigenia in Aulis* and *The Bacchae* are performed posthumously in Athens. Aristophanes' *The Frogs*, which features Aeschylus and Euripides in the underworld, is performed in Athens. Athens is surrounded by Spartan and Theban troops.
404	Athens capitulates, which brings an end to the Peloponnesian War. The enemy troops occupy the Acropolis.

401   Sophocles' *Oedipus at Colonus* is pro-
       duced posthumously at the dionysian
       theater.

399   Socrates is prosecuted and condemned to
       death.

THE AGE AND THE WORK

Athens

When Sophocles was six or seven, his native Athens was continuously alarmed at the prospect of an armed attack by the Persians. No doubt he sensed the approaching danger from the increased tension and agitation of the adults around him; later, decked with flowers, he was likely to have been among the crowds lining the streets as the victorious Athenian forces were jubilantly welcomed back from Marathon (490 B.C.). Ten years of peace followed, but every Athenian knew of the vengeance the Persian king, Xerxes, had vowed against their city.

While Sophocles was receiving the education usual for a son of a rich family and, in the ancestral gardens of Colonus just outside Athens, applying himself to science and the arts, to physical training and practice with weapons, it was current political events that caught his attention. It was the politics of a democracy that was still young, the first democracy of the Western world, the citizens of which spent the greater part of the day in the *agora*, the marketplace, where they conducted the business of self-government. In the decade after Marathon interparty strife was obscured by the fear of the Persians, who were again threatening Athens. Themistocles, the statesman charged with the city's defense and commander of its fleet, prevailed over the opposing factions and forged an alliance with the other Greek cities and provinces, above all with powerful Sparta, which controlled almost all of the Peloponnesus. For the moment, arguments and petty rivalries were silenced. The allied Greek army was led by the kings of Sparta (an aristocratic elite that was organized on almost communistic principles and that ruled this polis with an iron hand). The naval power was predominantly in the hands of Athens.

The events of 480 B.C. had an immense effect on the sixteen-year-old Sophocles. The Persian invaders approached by land and sea, preceded by all kinds of rumors. Xerxes mobilized the greatest army and fleet the world had ever seen. The enemy fired Greek cities, plundered and raped, and carried off inhabitants as slaves.

The Athenians decided to evacuate the city, leaving a force only on the Acropolis. Sophocles' family left Colonus and joined the great throng wending its way down to the harbor. For days the old, the children, the frail, and the slaves were ferried to the neighboring island of Salamis, the long mountain ridge of which was to be the camp for the main body of the Athenian forces. The fleet avoided an open-sea encounter with the enemy's vastly superior naval forces, and remained in the narrow strait between Salamis and the shore of Eleusis. (It was to the sacred hills of Eleusis that Athenians, with all the dignitaries in procession, made a pilgrimage every second spring and celebrated the great mysteries.)

To the east of Salamis lay Athens. The Acropolis was not yet covered with the buildings that were later to be so clearly visible from the distance, but it was even then the citadel and Athen's landmark. Young Sophocles stood among the lamenting Athenians as they looked across from Salamis and watched their city go up in flames. Out on the open sea the huge Persian fleet dropped anchor. Over in Eleusis the Athenians could make out the splendid and luxurious tent from which Xerxes directed operations. The main force of the Greek army had withdrawn to the isthmus of Corinth in order to block the entrance to the Peloponnesus. Most of the northeastern and eastern poleis at the tip of Boeotia had saved themselves from devastation through treaties with the Persians.

The situation was desperate. Xerxes had threatened to raze Athens to the ground and drag its citizens off to Asia as slaves. Next to Xerxes' tent was that of a deadly enemy of Greek democracy, Hippias, the son of the tyrant Pisistratos, who thirty years before had been overthrown and banished from Athens. The memory of his reign of terror was so fresh that many thought with horror of the bloody vengeance he would surely wreak among his foes—and most Athenians could be called that.

According to legend, after several days of nerve-racking delay, Themistocles finally managed to trick Xerxes through false intelligence into making the fatal mistake that cost the Persians their status as a great power. On receiving the false information that the Greek fleet would leave its position at the inlet the next night and slip out of his clutches, Xerxes gave the command to attack. As a result, from the hills of Salamis, the Athenians witnessed the spectacle of a rout unparalleled in history.

In the narrow strait the unwieldy Persian ships were completely outfought by the far more maneuverable

Athenian men-of-war. The victory was so incredible that the gods themselves were believed to have intervened, and word quickly spread that the flame of Eleusis—the light that appeared in the sky during the night of the mysteries—had been seen. After viewing the end of his fleet and his glory from a cliff on Eleusis, Xerxes fled, leaving his magnificent tent as booty for the victors to admire.

But the jubilation of the Greeks was cut short on their return to Athens. The smoldering ruins, the desecrated temples, the trampled gardens were to haunt Sophocles for the rest of his life. Eight years later the first of the great trio of tragic dramatists, Aeschylus, recalled the scene to the fading memories of his people when he portrayed on the stage not the exultation of the victors but the lamentations of the defeated. In *The Persians*, the oldest tragedy that we possess and the only one dealing with a contemporary event (it was produced in 472 B.C. when Xerxes was still alive), mothers and old people lament the loss of their sons, children the loss of their fathers, and kings the loss of their empires.

Poets felt that one of the functions of tragedy was to portray the horrors of war for a people all too readily inclined to forget them. They repeatedly and emphatically remind Athenians how easily a smoking Athens might have become a smoking Troy, from whose ruins no life ever again rose. Euripides, the youngest of the tragic playwrights, conveyed just such a message in his *Trojan Women*, and in *Ajax*, the earliest extant play by Sophocles, the chorus of Salaminian sailors standing before the walls of Troy chants: Cursed be the man who taught warfare to the Greeks.

But people have short memories. Soon after the end

of the Persian Wars, the Athenians indulged in a policy of imperialism. They extended their campaigns to Egypt; they made punitive raids on cities and islands that opposed the interests of the Athenian League. They dealt with their enemies, and those of their allies who proved disloyal, just as the Persians had once dealt with them. And at home the struggle for power among the parties continued unabated.

During his youth, Sophocles witnessed both the glory and the decline of great Athenians. For example, a year after leading the Greeks to victory at Marathon, Miltiades was threatened with being fined, a disgrace which only his death spared him. Twelve years after the end of the Persian Wars, Themistocles, who had engineered the victory at Salamis, was sent into exile. (He finished his days in Persia, where he was royally received.) After Themistocles' fall, his rival Cimon, son of the repudiated Miltiades, rose to power in Athens, but six years later Cimon was overthrown and exiled.

In spite of all, as a believer in democracy Sophocles still preferred "the hate-filled fighting of warring parties" to the terror imposed by one autocratic tyrant. He praised this struggle for power among men of equal rank as a test of the strength of freedom; he praised it with the passionate conviction of the Athenian who hated tyranny, dictatorship, and authoritarian rule. Politics formed the very essence of his life and the polis was at its center.

A Complete Education

The education of young Sophocles was that of an Athenian youth destined for public life. At the end of this curriculum were official positions, which were determined partly through elections and partly through the drawing of lots (so great was the fear that unscrupulous individuals might otherwise become powerful). But at the very beginning was a comprehensive education, the goal of which was a universality that hardly ever since has been repeated.

On the one hand, education consisted of political discipline in the narrow sense: military training above all, law, finance, government, and the rites of worship. It should occasion no surprise that the roles for officiation at religious rituals were studied by all: there was no established clergy in Athens, and the office of priest was conferred on citizens as a sign of respect. It was an office that anyone might take upon himself, and everyone had to be capable of carrying out the duties it entailed.

On the other hand, education also embraced those disciplines that now seem, though only at first glance, to be nonpolitical because they are not directly connected with politics. Sports was the most important of these disciplines, and victory at the Olympic games was an envied goal. There was also emphasis on the arts of music, poetry, dance, and the theater, but also subjects such as philosophy, mathematics, and astronomy.

The natural sciences were looked upon as arts: medicine, for example, was closely connected with music and the theater. The splendid theater of Epidaurus was erected (admittedly in postclassical times) near an Asclepieion, or a holy region, surrounding a therapeutic bath. A similar shrine to the god of medicine has been excavated not far from the Theater of Dionysus in Athens. Sophocles himself was said to have been connected with the introduction of the cult of Asclepios, in which he served as a priest.

The overlapping of the various disciplines in this way, surprising though it may seem to us today, was characteristic of the comprehensive education of that time. What Aristotle was later to define as part of the aim of tragedy—catharsis—is a medical term meaning purgation, a form of psychotherapy. Music theory, too, was closely associated with medical teaching concerning the emotions, while the mathematical genius Pythagoras was also the founder of a religious sect that believed in metempsychosis. Even more incredible things were said about Sophocles than that the honor of priesthood was bestowed on him in his old age. After his debut in the Theater of Dionysus (468 B.C.) when scarcely thirty years old, he was hailed as an actor of female roles (in the Greek theater of his time all roles were played by men). As Nausicaa in his own play that dealt with the episode of the Phaeacians in the *Odyssey*, he delighted his audiences by the girlish dexterity with which he played with the ball. In another of his early plays he achieved great success singing to lute accompaniment. Stranger still is the fact that by the time this artistically inclined man was fifty, we find him directing the financial affairs of the Athenian League. It was probably while he held this office—roughly equivalent to a contemporary secretary of the treasury—that he wrote *Antigone*.

But even that is not the end of the matter as far as his versatility and success are concerned. When Aeschylus had taken part in the battle of Marathon, he had only been a low-ranking officer (a fact that he wished to have immortalized on his epitaph, though no mention was to be made of his having been a dramatist!); but Sophocles was eventually made a *strategós* (general, or admiral). Although tradition has it that he did not distinguish himself in this position, he did have command in two campaigns. If we bear all this in mind, it is scarcely to be wondered at that he finally became a member of the ten-man probouleutic council, which, in times of trouble, ruled over the fate of the polis. In the Athens of that time, these varied forms of service could be part of a poet's life in the polis, of his life for the polis.

Life in the Polis

Conversely, however, all this belonged together: politics, art, military service, science, sports and worship were integral parts in the life of the polis. In the fifth century, B.C., during which tragedy blossomed and died, almost all the leading statesmen of Athens had received the kind of universal education described. Art was by its very nature public, an integral part of the whole. Pindar, the great poet, wrote his hymns for the Olympic games. The tragic poets of Attica wrote their plays for similar public festivals—the Dionysia.

When the citizenry shares so fully in the political aspects of public life, art more completely mirrors the age. This is especially true of the drama, which is the most public of all the arts. Athenian theater is clearly political theater, but it is more than just that. It is theological, philosophical, and moral theater. The process of development from the old to the new is mirrored in tragedy. But the thought behind this process is also mirrored. The tragic poets did not embrace the cause of any one party. Rather, they considered it their duty to remind everyone of the basic conditions of human existence, considerations that were often forgotten in the heat of political argument.

The old gods were still very much alive for Athenians. The state honored them in public ceremonies of worship—the festivals of the people were the festivals of the gods. And every child knew his Homer. The gods and heroes lived in the imagination in the vivid pictures in which the ancient epics, and later the artists, had depicted them.

Nonetheless, religious ideas had changed. Two opposing impulses gave rise to new trends. The first came from those strata of society that the aristocrats had tried to ignore. The more the common people rose up, the more powerfully the "new" gods made their presence felt. The new gods were, in reality, ancient, probably those of the original inhabitants who were once crushed by the Greeks as they surged over the land in three conquering waves. The worship of Dionysus—who was scarcely mentioned in Homer—unleashed a bacchantic frenzy that gripped the whole of Greece. The maenads took to the woods to celebrate their orgies. An act of liberation of irresistible power accompanied the rise of the common people to political equality.

It says much for the quality of the Greek mind that the state leadership was able to channel the flow of this eruption into ordered worship. The priests of the Delphic oracle had from time immemorial exercised a great influence on political life. They were invoked to sanction the constitutions that were now being registered everywhere, and they were commissioned to establish the cult of the new god, Dionysus. What the Dionysia meant for Athens and tragedy we will shortly see.

The powerful movement of the mysteries that were

celebrated by the Athenians in Eleusis may also be attributed to the Dionysian impulse, although there is no proof that the birth of Dionysus was the real mystery, as is often stated. (We do not know the secret; the initiated were sworn to secrecy, and death was the penalty for betraying that vow.) Here, too, the ancient gods of the people came to the fore, thrusting aside those emphasized in the Homeric world. There was renewed interest in Demeter, the earth mother, whose daughter Persephone had been snatched away by Hades and who had to spend a third of the year in the underworld—hence the myth of nature's seasons. As a result, the light that shone from Eleusis during the Sacred Night was thought to bring consolation to those who believed. Solon, the founder of democracy, fully recognized what such faith meant for men at a time when the Homeric gods were beginning to retire. He put the Eleusinian mysteries under the protection of the state.

The second impulse to give rise to new trends—an impulse that gripped the intellectuals in particular—was diametrically opposed to these irrational and emotional movements. It was the rise in importance of philosophy and science. When Thales predicted a solar eclipse in Miletus, the news spread over the whole of the Greek world, making it difficult to think of the sun as the god Helios, who drove his golden chariot across the heavens. A century and a half later the philosopher Anaxagoras, a contemporary and acquaintance of Sophocles', "blasphemously" maintained that the sun was a glowing ball of fire.

These new theories were as unsettling as Galileo's were to be 2000 years later. The age of enlightenment had begun. Gradually knowledge and experience were emphasized over faith. Heraclitus, known as "the Obscure," saw the essence of the world as lying in growth and decline ("everything is in flux"), while the principle that ruled it lay in the conflict between the powers of destruction and regeneration ("war is the father of all things"). He was the tragic philosopher. For him the gods were not anthropomorphic figures, as they had been for Homer (whom he wished to suppress), but inconceivable powers.

The effect of the Persian Wars on these movements was devastating. In the face of a huge death toll, the terror, and the destruction, the ability of the human intellect to control man's fate seemed highly questionable. But though the people were swept along on a new wave of religious fervor, the gods who had allowed such a terrible war disappeared still further into the distance. The pictures that still lived in the imagination no longer fitted the powers whose hammer blows now rained down on the suffering people.

In his last work, the *Oresteia*, Aeschylus undertook the huge task of placing the divine powers and human existence (the polis) into an order (the cosmos). The incomprehensibility of divine rule had given rise to the notion of the "quarreling gods." Just as Homer had put Hera on the side of the Trojans and Athena on the side of the Greeks, so now did Aeschylus equate the opposing powers with the disputing gods. And just as Sophocles was to have Aphrodite and Eros addressed as the irrational forces of love, and Ares invoked as the incomprehensible power of war, so too did Aeschylus pair off opposing forces.

In the *Oresteia*, for example, there is the conflict between Apollo, the Olympian god of the justice that demands expiation for the murder of a husband and king, and the Erinyes, the infernal goddesses of the justice that demands expiation of the matricide. Apollo, called on by the matricide Orestes, is unable to come to his assistance beyond referring him to Athena, who comes to a unique decision: she calls together a jury of mortals (this is the story of the founding of the Areopagus, Athens's judicial body) who are to decide the case.

It is of the deepest significance that the mortals are equally divided in their decision, so that Orestes is acquitted only through the tie-breaking vote of Athena. Litigation can no more be banished from the mortal world than can war or evil. But the divine idea of the polis, personified in Pallas Athena, is able to help men to live together in harmony—though only if they do not cease to "fear that which should be feared," or if they remain conscious at all times of the absolute limitation, the basic impasse that confronts all mortals.

After the Persian Wars

Immediately after the Persian Wars the conservative party of the aristocrats were initially in the majority in Athens. The radical democrats fought against the influence of the Areopagus in particular, since it represented aristocracy's last bastion of power. When the government would take no steps to curb the corruption that was rife among the highest judges, the leaders of the radical democrats decided to employ strength of arms. In 462 B.C. two young men of aristocratic family, Ephialtes and Pericles, seized power with the support of the people. With the Areopagus overthrown, there was no longer any limit on the power of the ruling party, and Ephialtes persecuted his enemies mercilessly, until he himself was murdered.

That this did not lead to the collapse of the revolution is due to the efforts of Pericles. Scarcely thirty at the time, he was destined to become the greatest Athenian statesman since Solon. Within a few years he had so strengthened his position that year after year he was elected to head the most important ministry, that of strategic warfare. As supreme commander of the armed forces, he was virtually absolute sovereign of the republic, and many objected that he ruled Athens like a tyrant; however, the means he employed were those of politics and not of terror. Submitting to democratic rule, he annually stood for re-election by the people's assembly, and he eliminated opposition by means of a majority vote.

Pericles is a figure of the greatest importance in any study of Sophocles. They were almost exact contemporaries, the poet being three years older. It is said, moreover, that they were friends, and most likely Pericles capitalized on the poet's reputation when he supported Sophocles' election to the post of finance minister.

In spite of all this, however, Sophocles was not a party liner subservient to the mighty man. On the contrary, he exercised his right to use the characters in his plays as a means to warn Pericles, if not to criticize him. As we shall see later, certain of Creon's traits, in *Antigone*, were unmistakably meant to suggest Pericles. Sophocles was here exercising a right Aeschylus had most emphatically insisted on. Four years after power had been wrested from the Areopagus, Aeschylus had the *Oresteia* produced. In this work Pallas

Athena places the rights of this judicial body above matters of daily politics and party strife. One can hardly dispute that there must have been a connection between such a blatant provocation of the ruling statesman and the emigration of the aged Aeschylus to Sicily, where he died in 456 B.C. Pericles was not yet strong enough to accept the kind of criticism he was later—perhaps with a smile—to allow Sophocles.

Aeschylus' admonitions were more than mere political criticism. For example, the oft-repeated "to fear that which should be feared," was directed against the attitudes that sprang up after Pericles came to power. People began to forget the horrors of the Persian Wars, and Pericles continued the imperialistic policies of his predecessors. He was determined to increase both the power of the polis he headed, and the respect in which it was held. One might say of him, as was earlier said of Ephialtes, that he "poured out the unadulterated wine of bourgeois freedom." And this is certainly true in that he continued to limit the power of the Areopagus.

Pericles became the guardian of worship and encouraged the arts, which blossomed as never before. Everything was done to the honor and glory of the state. Aeschylus had portrayed Pallas Athena as the personification of the ideal of the polis, but the statue of the goddess that Pericles commissioned from Phidias was larger than life and made of gold and ivory. Although it adorned the newly built Parthenon on the Acropolis, it was not the object of religious worship, and there was no divine service in the temple. Nor—judging from the accounts of Thucydides—were the gods ever mentioned in Pericles' speeches.

The task of the politician, according to Pericles, was

to do what was necessary. He was a man of calculating reason, and religion was for him an "anthropological fact" that he was forced to accept if he wanted to rule democratically. When his friend Anaxagoras was accused of blasphemy, there was nothing that Pericles could do about it. He associated with the philosopher Protagoras, whose celebrated "Man is the measure of all things" was the very basis of Sophist philosophy as we know it from Plato's Socratic dialogues.

We cannot say that the theory that "might is right" was foreign to Pericles, but we must also add that even if he voiced such cynicism in private, it did not characterize his public behavior. A great man is great not only because of what he is, but also because of the image he consciously projects. Pericles wanted his image to be that of a servant to the polis. He was never, despite his position of power, the polis itself, as Sophocles' Creon claims to be. It was never a case of "L'état c'est moi." But since the system of government practiced by Pericles was always in danger of degenerating into a dictatorship—and, indeed, in many instances seemed to be tyrannical or dictatorial—Sophocles felt justified in issuing the warning expressed from the stage in his *Antigone*.

Antigone was probably produced in 442 B.C. At the time there was peace in the land, and magnificent buildings glorified the polis. The audience in the Theater of Dionysus knew to whom they were indebted for the splendor of their new citadel. A chill must have run down their spines as they recognized in the tyrant Creon the traits that were intended to remind them of Pericles.

How different things looked in Athens when Sophocles' *Oedipus the King* was given its first performance. Pericles was dead. His memorial is Oedipus, a great man who put too much store in his own powers.

In 431 B.C. the Peloponnesian War with Sparta had broken out. (The end of this war, in 404 B.C., was to mark the fall of Athens.) The consequences of Pericles' imperialistic policies were evident. But yet another catastrophe had shaken the polis to its very foundations: pestilence. In the years 430 and 429 plague decimated the population of Athens. It is a bitter irony of the democratic ideal that the people now decided to depose their head of state—as if he could have been responsible for the plague!

Certainly nobody could have seriously accused Pericles of this, but was it not an error in his appraisal of the human condition that he made no allowances for calamities such as the plague? Had he not gone too far in pitting his own power against the superior power of the gods? Was he not guilty of hybris? Sophocles wrote his tragedy with a retrospective glance at the possibilities and limitations of the greatest human spirit, constructing an epitaph, an apology, a parable. *Oedipus the King* must have been produced soon after 429, the year in which Pericles died and the plague ran its course.

The great era of Athens ran inexorably towards its end. The aged Sophocles enjoyed the adoration of the people. It was at this time that a young writer of comedies came before the public eye. Aristophanes was barely twenty at the time his first plays were given. In his *The Frogs*, he brought Athens' great tragic dramatists onto the stage (the scene is set in Hades), by staging a terrible argument between Aeschylus and Euripides. Only Sophocles was spared, such was the veneration in which he was universally held. Seventy years old, the white-haired Sophocles passed through the streets of Athens, a legend in his own lifetime.

The passage of time dissolved the idea of the polis. With the advent of enlightened reason, as reflected on the stage in the dramas of Euripides, the interests of the individual superseded those of the general welfare to an ever greater extent. Politics became the method of playing off the interests of one group against those of another. The old ideals of justice, of public spirit, and of piety disappeared. In such a situation the adventurous plans of a fascinating genius, the youthful Alcibiades, thrived.

It was not possible for a new man simply to take over the legacy of Pericles. There were from time to time periods of stability, of stagnation, but radical changes occurred at ever closer intervals. Accordingly, Alcibiades was sometimes hailed as a victor, and then reviled as a loser. In 415 B.C. he succeeded in persuading the hard-pressed Athenians to stake everything on one venture: the Sicilian expedition. It was hoped that the riches of the Greek colonies on this island would compensate the city and the citizens for the losses they had suffered in recent years. The price paid for this hybris was terrible. The fleet and the expeditionary forces were annihilated. Not daring to return to Athens, Alcibiades sought refuge among its ememies, the Spartans.

Given their crushing defeat, Athenian citizens were temporarily inclined to discretion. Alcibiades was formally exiled, and the probouleutic council of ten, of which Sophocles, now eighty-three, was a member, was charged with the duties of government. But discretion was not destined to prevail, for in 413 B.C.

came revolution. Antidemocratic radicals toppled the probouleutic council and seized power. A macabre procedure characterized the decline of freedom. The historian Alfred Heuss writes:

> The people's assembly was transferred to Colonus, a little town just outside Athens. The people were driven there like so many sheep, surrounded by armed guards. . . . and there they voted unanimously to abolish democracy. . . . The demise of democracy coincided with a low point in the moral and political sphere that was not likely to be rivaled.

Sophocles had been born in Colonus, and here he set the scene of the action of his last play: *Oedipus at Colonus*. He was not destined to witness the play's production. The enemy already stood before the gates of Athens and the theaters were closed. In the year 406 B.C., the death of Euripides (at the age of seventy-one) might well have marked the last occasion before the collapse on which the Athenians gathered together in the Theater of Dionysus. The news of the death of the third of the great trio of tragic dramatists had reached Athens from Macedonia, for like Aeschylus, Euripides had died in exile. It is said on good authority that Sophocles entered the theater in mourning and that he had the actors wear mourning, too. This gesture, honoring his dead rival, was typical of the spirit which placed universal good higher than that of the individual, which esteemed the polis more than the parties, and for which the tragedy counted for more than the tragedian.

The last of the 123 plays that Sophocles wrote—only seven have come down to us—were written in the shadow of Athens' decline. *Electra* was written during the years in which he was *probulos*. It was probably conceived as an answer to Euripides' *Electra*, which had just been performed. Sophocles' play portrays the heroic in opposition with the all-too-human by means of two characters, one of whom, Orestes, is presented as the direct opposite of Alcibiades. *Philoctetes* is the tragedy of a suffering hero, forsaken by gods and mortals alike, who is redeemed when a god persuades him to serve the common good. *Oedipus at Colonus*, a mystery play intended as a revision of his earlier *Oedipus the King*, portrays the redemption of another suffering hero, as his living corpse is received into the polis of the golden age—into Athens as it had once been.

These last plays do not concern the hero as a man of action. The suffering Electra is clearly of greater importance than her brother Orestes, the man of action. Philoctetes' companion in arms, Neoptolemus, the son of Achilles, is not a heroic type but simply a person in whom justice prevails over reason—compassion and virtue over political expediency. It is readily understandable that the Athens into which the ideal sovereign Theseus receives the suffering Oedipus is the old polis in which justice counts as the highest good. It is equally apparent that Sophocles is now more kindly disposed to his heroes.

The power of the gods should not be seen only in the cruel blows with which they destroy human might and greatness but also in the way they make justice prevail on earth after much suffering. Those who suffer are heroic because they refuse to give in to the blows of the gods and the pressures exerted on them by their fellow humans. Unlike their fellows, they do not conform or acquiesce, but by suffering they survive and overcome. Thus, they realize a rare possibility of human existence, and after death they receive a reward that raises them above ordinary mortals.

The Greeks believed—and this belief found expression in the cult of the hero—that fame meant immortality. This was a simple conclusion arrived at with no recourse to mystical or romantic longing. The immortality of Achilles, Theseus, Orestes, Heracles, Oedipus, and Antigone is inferred from the fact that they continue to live in the minds of men. Because posterity celebrates and honors those heroes who once suffered, their fame continues from age to age. And this undoubtedly was what inspired the aged Sophocles to wrap an aura of compassionate tenderness, of sanctity, around his suffering heroes.

The gods destroy both the guilty and the innocent in this world. The higher one climbs, the farther one falls. "All creation is subject to their whiplash," Heraclitus said of the gods, and this is the fundamental tragedy of our existence. The function of tragedy is to tear aside the veil of appearance that obscures the very essence of life from ordinary men and to make them conscious of the deeper truth of existence. Sophocles' last plays portray the tragic hero with an aura that shines into posterity and bestows immortality upon those who suffer.

Sophocles died in 405 B.C., one year after Euripides. He was spared the harrowing experience of having to witness the capitulation of Athens in 404. It is reported that the Spartans, upon hearing the news of the poet's death, offered the besieged city safe conduct for the funeral procession to the cemetery, which lay outside the city walls.

When, five years later, *Oedipus at Colonus* was given its first performance in the Theater of Dionysus by Sophocles' grandson, there was a Spartan garrison on the Acropolis. The end of the free polis also marked the end of the golden age of tragedy.

THE STAGE AND TRAGEDY

The Theater

In March and April of each year the Athenians celebrated the Greater Dionysia—one of the festivals of Dionysus, whose significance we have already touched upon. This god of ecstasy and metamorphosis, this god of the theater, was also the god of wine, and the Greater Dionysia was probably held in celebration of the grape harvest, and Athenians generously sampled the new wine that flowed freely from the casks. It was at such a festival that Thespis, the reputed founder of tragic drama, is said to have driven his cart into the city from a nearby vineyard and made his first appearance on the stage. Before this there had been choruses of singers and dancers, and it was from such a chorus, thought to have been clad in goatskins, that we get the word tragedy—*trag-odia*, or goat's song. But the precise origin and development of the theater is clothed in obscurity.

It is known that the tyrant Pisistratus raised the simple festival of a folk god to the status of a national festival (like all tyrants, he sought the support of the people in the struggle against the aristocracy). The traditional date given for Thespis' first stage appearance is 534 B.C., which coincides with the reign of the tyrant. The festival survived the tyrants. When democracy was restored, the plays that climaxed the Dionysia were so popular that the Athenians felt compelled to find a better location for them. So they built the "old temple" on the south side of the Acropolis at the edge of an extensive grove of olive trees. The foundations of this temple were discovered by archeologists not far from the "new temple," built much later.

A grassy hollow in the slope of the Acropolis created a natural amphitheater that could accommodate thousands. Later, terraced seats were cut into the soil, and even later still, wooden benches were provided. It was apparently when these benches collapsed during a performance of a play by Aeschylus that the decision was made to build a more permanent structure. But even then the seats were constructed of wood; the stone spectator area, as well as all the other ruined sections that we can see today, dates from the postclassical era. Indeed, we have only a very vague idea of what the theater must have looked like in classical times. (By classical, we refer to that period between 472 B.C., first performance of Aeschylus' *The Persians*, and 401 B.C., when Sophocles' *Oedipus at Colonus* was first staged.) Based largely on conjecture, drawn from existing ruins, the value of this mental image is disputable.

Accommodating between 14,000 and 17,000 spectators, the Theater of Dionysus was huge even by today's standards. Though it was by no means large enough to contain the entire population, it was nonetheless definitely the theater of the polis. The multitude must have swelled with pride in their city. Behind the seated spectators rose the Acropolis. The architectural wonders admired by present-day tourists were built during this classical era of tragedy: the Parthenon (probably dedicated shortly after the first performance of *Antigone*), the Propylaea, the Erechtheum, and the Temple of Victory. Statues of unmatched beauty adorned the citadel—Phidias was the general supervisor of the artists who worked on the Acropolis. If we wish to picture for ourselves the actors and choruses of classical tragedy, we need only look at the figures of the gods and heroes, at the bas-reliefs of the battles and the processions in the pediments and metopes of these buildings; we need only look at those completed at the same time on the Zeus temple in Olympia, or at the bronze statue of Poseidon, which was recently found in the sea off Cape Artemision.

With their backs to the Acropolis, the Athenians could look upon the sea, which they considered their own. (The site had been chosen for this very reason.) The land of Attica is bare and not very fertile, and from earliest times the sea therefore had an attraction for this busy people. Sea and trade soon became the source of the power and the wealth of the polis. Everyone had traveled by ship, many had served in the navy, and some owned ships that transported goods (mostly arms and tools) into the wide world and brought back a variety of imports. During the classical period all theaters had this view of the sea. In many of the extant tragedies the sea plays a significant role—the heroes' ships lie at anchor in the harbor, or the people wait for their return from journeys or wars across the seas.

To the left and right of the sea rise mountains and hills, for the most part bare and gray. But just behind the theater there were groves and gardens stretching down to the sea. The "treasure of the land," the leafy olive trees, glimmered like silver in the green of the landscape. And above this green and silver, above the blue of the sea shimmering away into the distance, was the great vault of the blue sky, out of which the sun shone brighter than anywhere else in the world. Even in the springtime the sun was so hot that by noon the plays, which were begun in the early morning, had to be interrupted. The audience retired to the shade of the trees or returned to the city for their midday meal. Later on, long colonnaded halls were erected, and here the people were able to rest and take refreshment. On returning to the amphitheater in the afternoon, Athenians again saw the irresistible silver and green superimposed on the interminable blue.

The quality of the light in Greece is unforgettable. People speak of its crystal clarity, but even this description is inaccurate, for there seems to be nothing between the viewer and what he is looking at. As one recedes from an object, it scarcely seems to diminish in size, and even at great distances the eye can distinguish fantastic details. There is no blurring of the images such as we see in impressionist paintings. Even from the top of the Acropolis one can see the actors in the theater distinctly; it is almost as if the clearly cut figures of the friezes had come to life and were walking about. No matter where one sat in the amphitheater, at either side or at the back, one had a perfect front-seat view. Mere numbers cannot express this nearness any more adequately than mathematics can convey the magnificence of the Parthenon, in which for optical reasons the columns are out of mathematical sym-metry. With such clarity of light, the actors were more immediate, more close to the audience than they were on any other stage in the world.

This sense of proximity was not only visual, but stemmed from the acoustics of the ancient theaters, which were nothing short of miraculous. The secret of these wonderful acoustics has never been fully ex-plained. From the very last row one can hear every work of a normal converstion held on the stage. The delicate sound of a flute, of a whisper, can be heard throughout the whole amphitheater. A fourth dimen-sion seems to be added to the three dimensions of sight. It is as though ancient statues were speaking. There is a nearness and a fullness in the scene that is so extraordinary as to be hardly natural. But such rich and full unity of sound and sight only occurs when the audience listens and watches with extreme concen-tration, totally cutting off all other sounds and sights. With complete silence and a complete lack of distrac-tion, the play can begin.

It was not only the play to which the audience felt so closely linked. They also felt close to each other. Looking down onto the stage one was conscious of the many thousands of heads; since the plays took place in daylight, one was always aware that a performance was being given. Nobody could fall into a trance and confuse the action on the stage with reality. And yet the audience was always prepared to identify with the feelings, thoughts, and passions expressed before them; they were always prepared to empathize.

Since they almost always knew the outcome of the play, the spectators were more interested in *how* everything was done than in *what* was done. They were preoccupied with how the dramatist treated his material and how it was portrayed on the stage. Indeed, they saw the material and its presentation almost as one, since the dramatist himself usually directed his play and, in the early classical period, acted in it as well. We find no stage directions in the texts of extant plays.

Only with the actual production did the play reach its finished form. The dramatists considered music and dance as elements in their plays, and gave as much thought to them as to the mime of the actors. Language was only a part of a grand unified work of art. The different elements did not merge into one; they were not drowned in a Wagnerian sea of music. Instead, the plays resembled those of the great Asiatic theaters. The dramatist's mastery was demonstrated by the way he was able to combine the various elements, by the originality with which he composed his work.

The musical sections of the work—the orchestra with chorus, the complex choreography—were distinctly and logically separated from the spoken section. As there was no curtain, entrances and exits were an important part of the production. The critical audience concentrated on the structure of the play, since the action was well known to them, and the dramatists did their best to introduce novelties. This was often done by means of short scenes and the use of processions. The visual spectacle was every bit as important as the spoken word. The Greek word *théatron*, which was originally used simply for the spectator area, actually means "seeing place."

One further reason the audience was so interested in how the events were presented was that their critical judgment of the play was an important element of the occasion. The festival was really a contest (*agón*). The dramatists submitted their plays, and a jury selected certain of them for performance. It was the audience, however, that awarded the prizes. There were, of course, official critics, but their task was to ascertain the effect on the audience. On each of three days of the festival, a given dramatist would be represented by three plays, followed by a farcical epilogue in the form of a satyr play. The term "satyr play" is derived from the chorus of goat-footed satyrs in shaggy skins who took possession of the stage when the tragedians had left it. There are fragments of a satyr play by Sophocles extant, a sort of joke predominantly in dance form, entitled *The Trackers*.

Initially the three plays were in the form of a trilogy. Only one such example is extant: Aeschylus' *Oresteia*. Though Sophocles used this as a model, his three plays treated three different subjects and three different heroes, and were followed by the satyr play. The longest of the three plays was presented first, beginning at about eight in the morning and lasting about two and a half hours. The other two plays were about two hours. They were given in the afternoon with a short interval between them. Torches were probably lighted during the satyr play, and often during the final scenes of the preceding play.

After the third day, first-, second-, and third-place prizes were awarded. The names of the prize winners were engraved on marble tablets, some of which still exist today. Sophocles won the first prize on eighteen occasions. But his greatest play, *Oedipus the King*—perhaps the greatest tragedy of all time—was never popular with an audience. Of all the plays by Sophocles, none ends with quite such an air of hopelessness, none moves quite so inexorably toward its tragic conclusion.

One astonishing clause in the rules for the contest was that each author was compelled to submit totally new plays. None of the tragic writers ever saw a play of his performed a second time in the Theater of Dionysus. The new productions of Aeschylus' plays were allowed only after his death, and then, of course, they were not presented for competition.

The texts of prize-winning plays were recorded by the state; however, these plays were "revived" only by theaters in other cities. Delegations from allied states and envoys from foreign powers always attended the festivals and shared the front rows of the theater with the archons, or holders of high office. But the imposing armchairs, which can still be seen in the Theater of Dionysus, are from a later date. It goes without saying that during the classical period no seat could be superior to another.

Although the costs of a production were always borne by a rich citizen of the city, the *choragús*, there was an admission charge. Pericles introduced a law whereby lower income groups were allowed free admission. The tokens given out for this purpose represent one of the earliest examples of a state subsidy for the theater.

The Chorus

Without doubt, it is the chorus that most obviously distinguishes classical tragedy from contemporary theater. (Our opera is more akin to classical tragedy than is modern drama. Indeed, opera emulates tragedy in its use of the chorus and in other respects, too.) Modern drama, with its emphasis on the spoken word, is a relatively late development. Even comedy, which developed in Athens somewhat later than the tragedy and had its own festival, used the chorus in its classical form, represented by Aristophanes.

It is true that the chorus gradually lost its initial importance. Sophocles stands more or less in the middle of this development. In his plays the chorus still has powers of expression, but it is usually shorter and less lyrical than in Aeschylus' dramas, for example. Euripides pushed the chorus further and further into the background, and the trend that led to Menander's comedies, which are mostly spoken—and spoken, moreover, by single voices—began to appear in outline.

The chorus was one of the original elements in the composition of the tragic "total theater." It remained in existence as an independent genre, separate from the theater. Great poets and musicians wrote in this form, and there were concert halls for choral presentations, such as the Odeon near the Dionysian Theater. Like tragedy, this form was included among the contests of the Greater Dionysia.

Originally, the chorus probably consisted of fifty singers standing in a circle in the midst of the audience. This circle remained the true center of the Theater of Dionysus, and is probably a fairly true indication of its original form. This central area is known as the orchestra and is almost enclosed by the amphitheater. "Drama" (meaning "action" in Greek) came into being when one of the singers stepped before the rest of the chorus as a leader or soloist in order to speak to them or answer their questions. The Greek word for actor really means "responder."

This solo voice has behind it a tradition that goes back to the reciter, or rhapsodist of the Homeric epic; it is also the source of the great art of lyric poetry (that of Sappho, for example). We should not equate the introduction of a solo voice with the origin of dialogue any more than we should consider the chorus as purely musical (as it is in our opera, for example). The soloist was from the very beginning both singer and speaker, and the chorus was never so "musical" that every single word could not be clearly distinguished.

There was one further element essential to the chorus as we find it in the tragedy. This element seems to have been of decisive importance, for from it, as we have seen, came the word tragedy itself. It is the dance performed in costume and masks. These dances were executed only by the performers, but there were, in addition, round dances in which the audience participated. Older than the masked dances, they continued to be performed after the newer form developed.

But it was only in the masked dances—and this quite early—that the mimical elements of transformation developed along two lines: sudden terror and jubilation, the demonic and the farcical. Both elements have become integral parts of the Greek theater. The fear that Aeschylus' demonic Erinyes inspired in the audience is documented. In the satyr play, however, the aim was to complement the tragedies by providing pure delight. (They had a function similar to that of the *kyogen* interludes in the Noh theater, and the intermezzos in the baroque theater.)

Even before the development of tragedy, mime had

given rise to a separate theatrical form: the *mímos*. Jesters traveled through the country giving performances at the fairs and in the marketplaces. They performed conjuring tricks, played the buffoon, satirized current events, and travestied those in power. Writing at the same time as Aeschylus and Sophocles, two poets of the *mímos* form achieved great fame: Epicharmus and Sophron.

We know little about them, but we can say that neither the satyr play nor the comedy could have developed as they did without the influence of the mime. The genre persisted to the very end of classical Greece, and toward the close of the era even eclipsed the other forms of theater. The great mimes were as celebrated as modern film stars.

All this played its part in the performance that took place on the circular song and dance area in the orchestra, where the chorus held sway. The musicians probably sat here; though few in number, owing to the incredible acoustics, they were as effective as a modern orchestra. We have already mentioned that the musical theory of the ancients was based on the medical and scientific teaching of the effects of music. Each instrument was thought to have a particular emotional effect—the flute created delight, the lyre solemnity, as percussion instruments beat out the rhythm. But we have little idea of how this music actually sounded.

In Sophocles' tragedies there are two main types of choral song: the primary song and the antiphonal song. The primary song was sung by the members of the chorus in accompaniment to rhythmical dance steps. The choreography varied in mood from the restrained to the excited and even orgiastic.

It has been established that Sophocles raised the number of singers in the chorus from twelve to fifteen. This may point to the growing artistic interest in symmetry, since fifteen allows for an arrangement of two rows of seven and a chorus leader who may often have functioned as a solo voice in the dialogue sections. Moreover, seven was the principal of the mystical numbers (in which Pythagoras himself believed). In any case, we may be sure that the Greeks, for whom proportion played such an important role, were aware of the symmetrical and proportional possibilities of the numbers involved.

Sophocles' chorus always has a dramatic function, and it often interrupts the action. It usually has a definite and clearly defined character. Sometimes it represents the council of elders—the *Gerousía* of the early Greek states—voicing the opinion of the people and urging caution. Sometimes the chorus is composed of young girls, women, and soldiers and simply represents the people (the *polloí*), those who think and speak on a level different from that of the hero. Sophocles is the most objective of the tragic poets. We never hear his opinion through the individual speeches, but we sense it from the meaning behind the whole tragedy.

The chorus is neither the voice of the audience nor that of the dramatist. Psychologically it stands between the audience and the hero, a fact symbolically represented by its physical position in the orchestra. One of its main functions is to convey to the audience by means of emotional music the moods of the dramatic situation. In the same way, the often profound thoughts embedded in the words of the chorus are transmitted to the spectators for reflection. But the audience is never obliged by suggestion or persuasion simply to accept what is put before it. The chorus never formulates what the audience should think but simply sets the thought processes in motion—it engages the sympathy of the spectators.

In a similar fashion, the chorus prepares the audience for what is about to take place. A premonition of catastrophe or jubilation at the approach of some happy event is contained in the song or can be detected in the movements of the dance. At times the chorus serves to suspend time or to make it move faster.

Images and myths are conjured up as metaphors for what is felt and thought—and feelings and thoughts are almost always linked. The fifteen members of the chorus did not express themselves as one unit, as our modern opera choruses do, nor did they move in the identical steps of a well-rehearsed corps de ballet. Each member had to allow the feeling or thought to develop spontaneously within him. He then bodily expressed it in what seemed to him to be a proper form. (We never come across the word "we" in the chorus; it is always "I.") Accordingly, the director or choreographer gave only the broadest outline of what he required from the chorus. To some extent he was able to let things take their course because the songs and dances were all based on traditional models and received the particular slant necessary only within the context of the dramatic situation.

Whether they expressed grief or joy, all gestures were based on those the individual might have used in real life. The director simply combined the varied, but basically similar actions. The effect must have been like that conveyed by the Parthenon friezes in which the men, women, and children representing the people all have individual traits and yet are still part of a rhythmically proportioned whole. The choral song was usually divided into sections, each containing a strophe and an antistrophe. Sophocles' great art as a poet can be seen from the way he refused to let the strophic form determine his content. He arranged for the content to rise to a climax that demands the strongest and clearest expression before a precipitous drop is introduced. This is precisely how the modern poet deals with the traditional forms he has inherited.

In spite of innovations, the choral song retained an archaic character right up to the last classical tragedies. It was written in the Doric dialect—unfamiliar to the Athenian ear and was therefore immediately distinguishable from the rest of the text by its timbre alone. The dialogue was in the Attic dialect and sounded more or less like normal conversation, though in metrical form. The choral song was clearly intended to be raised above everyday language.

As tragedy developed further and further away from its origins, the chorus too diminished in importance. But Sophocles was conscious of the fact that this dramatic device could be, and should be, an essential element of tragedy. For the traditional is always part of the present; the past never completely dies out, and not everything that is old is doomed to pass into obscurity. In Sophocles' day, Homer was still very much part of the present and Athens was filled with old statues and temples. The people still made pilgrimages to the graves of dear and illustrious ancestors in the cemetery just outside the city. The closer to his contemporaries the poet tried to bring the old myths, the more clearly he wished to demonstrate that the theater and tragedy could be relevant to contemporary life only so long as the people recognized the importance of preserving the beauty of the past. It was on a par with continuing to worship Apollo at Delphi, with congregating for the Panhellenic Games at Olympia.

Compared with those of Aeschylus, Sophocles' tragedies represent a tremendous innovation without detracting from the earlier dramatist's achievement. Such innovation shows only one thing; that the traditional, the old, only lives on if it is rejuvenated. Sophocles did not dispense with the old and set up something new in its place. He simply gave new form to what already existed. We know that this was the way his thoughts ran; we know, too, that he foresaw a time when the old would no longer have the same meaning for people that it did for him. The chorus of the Old Men of Thebes prophesies this time in *Oedipus the King*:

> If all this perishes, if such deeds are held in honor,
> Why then should I honor the gods in song and dance?
> —The gods are fading away.

The traditional characteristics of the choral song—which disappear when the chorus joins in the dialogue (in Attic dialect), or takes up a dramatic function—have given rise to the opinion, unfortunately still current today, that tragedy not only had its origin in cult, but is by its very nature cultic and must therefore be played in a ritualistic manner.

Obviously, the cultic was one of the elements contributing toward the rise of tragedy, which originated as part of the Dionysia. But this was only *one* of many contributory factors. Cult and theater had existed side by side from very early times and continued to do so in the classical age. The cult made use of theatrical elements, and the theater absorbed aspects of the cult.

Where cult and theater coincide is in the presentation of events by means of actors, and it is precisely here that we are able to make a clear distinction between them. The cultic was invariable.

An integral part of the ritual of the Eleusinian mysteries were the presentations of sacred episodes. They were always identical in content, just as the central episodes in the mystery plays of medieval times were always identical. Each performance might vary slightly in the form of presentation and in minor details (just as the music changes from one composer's mass to another's), but the events themselves remained invariable. Since the mystery was always the same it was well known to everyone from beginning to end. The events were sacred, and their presentation fixed by canon. The same cannot be said of tragedy.

We have already pointed out that the earliest tragedy we possess, Aeschylus' *The Persians*, treats of a contemporary event; the defeat of the Persians at Salamis. It is far removed from cultic sanctity if only because the setting of the play is among the Persians and their gods. There were many similar plays in earlier times. The stories of those plays based on the myths were certainly well known to the audience, but the theatergoers were not particularly interested in the mythological content. Their interest lay in the new presentation and new interpretation given the story by the dramatist, whose intention was to move them so that this new rendering of the old seemed a representation of their own lives.

There was no question of cult here. The audience was not exhorted to offer up pious prayers but to think. Each of Sophocles' tragedies leads the spectator to a slowly dawning new insight. If the tragedies given at the Dionysian festival had not all possessed some kind of novel value that would appeal to the critical faculties of the audience, there could have been no contest. Who can critically appraise a ritual?

Because there is much talk of the gods in Sophocles, his work has often been termed "religious theater." But if this were so, Goethe's *Faust* would also be a religious play. One might just as well call Sophocles' plays political theater, for they are as much concerned with the polis as with the gods. In point of fact, his tragedies are both religious and political, but, as we shall see, even this description does not convey their essence.

The Stage

Thespis, who is said to have invented dialogue when he stepped out of the chorus as soloist, may well have been responsible for a second innovation on the Greek stage. When performances were given in market-places, there was a need for a raised platform, so that the soloist could be seen over the heads of the chorus. It is quite possible that Thespis' cart served as an impromptu stage.

The Greek word for stage, *skené*, really means "tent." A tent may have been put up alongside or behind the cart to serve as a dressing room or storage area. Because of the word's meaning it was long assumed that the Theater of Dionysus originally had some sort of tentlike stage area, which continued to be called the *skené* when the structure later became more permanent. This idea is generally discredited today. One can easily see that the "tent" could have been erected *behind* the stage, thus remaining hidden from the audience. We can still see today how steeply the grove slopes down behind the stage, and it is generally accepted that any dressing rooms or storerooms were situated here during the days of classical drama.

It is almost certain that the stage was one or two steps higher than the orchestra. The positioning of this stage as a sort of tangent to the circular orchestra area resulted in two "wings" stretching out on either side. These wings had steps running the full length. This arrangement of the stage into the *skené* with its two *paraskénia*, or side wings, is by no means absolutely certain, but it seems more than probable.

At a relatively early time supporting walls must have been built at each end of the amphitheater's terraced seats. The gaps between these walls and each end of the stage was probably utilized as an entrance for all those actors who did not enter from the middle of the stage. The chorus, above all, must have entered through this aperture. The opening song of the chorus took its name from the Greek word for corridor: *párodos*.

Originally the orchestra was simply a circle stamped out in the earth. Later separated from the audience by a ditch into which rain could drain, it was paved with flagstones. (The marble paving that can be seen today dates from a later period.) The stage developed along similar lines. It was originally of wood. Just exactly when it was paved with breccia stone is a matter of some dispute, but it was probably before the end of the classical era.

In the fourth century, a marble pavement was laid

over the stone foundation, and in the same period the stonework of the terraces was completed. A palacelike stone facade was constructed for the *skené*, and henceforth utilized in all plays. This facade had a large central portal and smaller portals in the two projecting side wings. If there had ever been a similar structure during the classical era, it was probably made of wood and served as a decoration that could be removed or changed whenever a particular play demanded it. That this must have been true may be seen from the last two plays by Sophocles, which both demand a *skené* with a particular view: *Philoctetes* calls for a cave in some rocks, and *Oedipus at Colonus* for an olive grove.

It is clear, therefore, that some sort of removable decor, some kind of scene change, was commonly used for tragedies in the classical era. The scenic devices were probably more practical and more realistic than is commonly supposed. Sophocles' earliest play, *Ajax*, requires an empty stage with a tent. There is no doubt that this was a commander's tent, which was moved to one side (probably on rollers) during the performance, for the last act is set in an open field "near the sea." *Antigone*, *Oedipus the King*, and *Electra* probably all made use of a palacelike facade and the *paraskénia*, a set that had been popular at least since Aeschylus' *Oresteía*. In *The Women of Trachis*, Heracles' house was simpler—he was an exile—and probably lacked the projecting side wings.

Documents are available to us testifying that the great artists of the day cooperated in the design of the sets. It is said that Sophocles greatly encouraged the use of painted scenery, and wooden screens were no doubt used for this purpose. The rocky cave of Philoctetes was probably done in this way, or the rock to which Prometheus was secured in Aeschylus' *Prometheus Bound*.

Painting was also used to depict rocks, and the palacelike facade was also decorated in this way. (We should note that the facade was really a very solid affair: people seated in the higher seats at the back of the amphitheater could look down on the roof.) *Oedipus at Colonus*, Sophocles' last play, seems to show a reversion to an earlier lack of decor. The stage was as empty as in the earliest plays by Aeschylus. The only decoration was one of nature's: the grove behind the *skené*, into which the hero vanished so mysteriously.

The tragic dramatists had only one spotlight—the sun. But they certainly knew how to use it. Its passage across the heavens played a large role in those plays given in the mornings, and those long drawn-out shadows that fell across the theater in the evenings were actually part of the dramatist's plans. We must also consider the effect of the sunlight when it shone toward the audience from behind the stage. In *Oedipus the King*, written for morning performance, the sun would have been directly behind the stage when the blinded Oedipus stepped from the door of the palace; the facade, like the figure of the hero himself, would have been in the shadow, but the whole scene would have an aura of light around it.

Aeschylus is thought to have favored mechanical stage devices, whereas Sophocles had little use for them. Some of Aeschylus' plays are unthinkable without the high cranes that lowered the gods to the stage. Athena in Sophocles' *Ajax* may well have stood next to the mortals on the stage, her invisibility being demonstrated by having the actors behave as if she were not there. But provision was made for divine visitations by providing a raised platform, the *theologeión*, or the "gods' speaking place." It is therefore possible that the actor playing Athena mounted some stairs behind the tent decor in order to appear on the *theologeión*. At the end of *Philoctetes* Heracles appears as a god: he probably stood on the *theologeión* amid the jagged points of the rocks.

Another mechanical device, known as the *eccýclema*, was a small, square platform that could be pushed onto the open stage of rollers from the midst of the scenic structures. Sophocles probably used this device only in his earlier plays. The *eccýclema* was normally used to convey dead bodies out into the center of the stage after a battle, or some other bloody event, had taken place. By means of this contrivance, in *Ajax*, the bloodspattered but triumphant hero was brought onto the stage, surrounded by the dead cattle he had slaughtered in the mistaken idea that they were his enemies.

Later Sophocles dispensed with the use of the *eccýclema*, but he did not spare his audience such gruesome sights. Instead, he simply made them part of the dramatic action. In *Antigone*, for example, Creon carries his son, who has just committed suicide, onto the stage. In *The Women of Trachis*, Heracles, racked by dreadful pain because of the poison smeared on his robe, throws off all covering in order to reveal to the bystanders (and the audience) his poison-pitted body. In *Electra*, Orestes, after he has killed Clytemnestra, forces Aegisthus, her lover and her accomplice in the murder of Agamemnon, to lift the shroud and view the bloody corpse. Theater at this time shows a predilection for such powerful and unforgettable spectacles set against a background of rather bare and bleak scenery.

The Actors

These spectacles and the scenery depended, of course, on actors whose behavior was lifelike rather than ritualistic. But, one may well ask, how can the use of mask be reconciled with the notion of living people? It is, in fact, precisely this point that has given rise to a fundamental misunderstanding of the nature of Greek theater.

One usually thinks of the mask as being similar to those we often see used in modern productions of classical plays: made of metal or some such inflexible material; the hair a mere imitation, as rigidly fixed as the rest of the mask; the mouth torn open in a suitably tragic expression. Such masks have, of course, become the symbol of the theater. But, in dealing with Aeschylus, Sophocles, and Euripides we must forget this stereotyped mask. It was not introduced until much later, when tragedy itself had become a rigidly fixed and archaic form in which the characters were as lifeless as the masks themselves.

It is these later masks that are seen in museums, for not a single genuine mask from classical times has survived. The masks used in the early performance of classical tragedy were made of perishable material. Soft enough to be drawn over the face, they had wigs of real hair firmly fixed to them. The mask was painted—Aeschylus is said to have introduced this custom, the intention being to make the mask more natural. (Tradition has it that Thespis had worn white makeup; for this reason the fabric of the mask was originally left white.)

The function of the mask was to hide the actor's own features and substitute those suited to the role he was to play. But underneath the painted mask, one could still detect a distinctly human face. (We may draw a parallel here between the actors' masks and the figures of the gods and mortals sculpted by Phidias and his school: underlying the particular quality identifying the character or god, there was an individual human quality.) The "alienating" effect of the mask was only such as was required by the verse which was clearly more elevated than everyday language.

The mask, then, was not ritualistic, it was not a mere archaism, and it did not strive for idealization. Its function was a heightening of effect. By obscuring the features of the actor's own face, the mask enabled the actor to "grow into" the character represented by the mask and to become this character unequivocally and unmistakably. The clearcut delineation of character facilitated by the mask was an absolute necessity for one very practical reason. The thousands of spectators all had to be able to recognize clearly, even from the very back row, the role being portrayed.

The function of these clearly delineated masks becomes even more obvious when we realize that certain roles required several masks. Antigone, for example, had a second mask that she wore as she was led off to her underground prison. Its hair was cropped short. And when Oedipus returned from the palace after having blinded himself, he wore a mask in which two black holes had been burned, and drops of blood could be seen running down the cheeks.

Like the metal masks, the *cothurnus* was also a later

invention. It was a kind of shoe reaching as high as the calf, and it had a sole eight inches or more thick. Wearing this shoe, the actor appeared larger than life. The significance of the *cothurnus* has also been misinterpreted. From contemporary vase paintings we can see that the shoes worn by actors during the classical period were scarcely raised at all. Where the sole had been adapted, it is no thicker than the soles of the shoes worn by modern actors who want to appear somewhat taller. It is possible that only those actors playing heroes wore such slightly raised shoes, since they were meant to appear taller than the people in the chorus or the actors of minor roles; however, it seems more likely that the heroes were simply played by actors who were actually somewhat taller.

Just as the mask had an intensifying effect, so also did the costumes of the principal characters raise them above the everyday. But here, too, Sophocles was responsible for a change of emphasis; costuming became dramatically determined and was used as a means of characterization. We therefore find Clytemnestra, the queen, dressing her daughter Electra as a slave. The fallen or damned heroes present a lamentable picture because of what they wear. Philoctetes, cast away on Lemnos because of the stench from the wound in his foot, is covered with filthy rags. Oedipus, worn by his long years of pilgrimage and deprivation, is likewise in rags in *Oedipus at Colonus*. Theseus, on the other hand, resplendent in the hero's costume, is the very epitome of a ruler.

As can be seen in the vase paintings, costume was also important in communicating character and fate. Queens, for example, appeared in purple robes embroidered with gold and silver trappings of royalty.

Stage properties were of great importance: weapons above all, but also sacrificial offerings, ribbons and garlands, the royal scepter (a long staff), the bent staff of the seer or that of the wanderer. The wanderer was immediately recognized by his staff and wide-brimmed sun hat. He traditionally entered from the right, for the sea, which represented distant regions for the audience, lay to the right of the theater. An entry from the left signified that the character was arriving from the city, for that was, indeed, where Athens lay. Part of the audience could see anyone entering from this side for some distance, so it was intentionally arranged for the chorus to walk in a procession when making its entrances and exits. Moreover, it was not only the chorus that entered as a procession. There were in all plays larger and smaller processions consisting of major characters with supernumeraries—bodyguards, servants and maids, military escorts (the Greek term *pompé* survives in our own word "pomp").

The number of soloists was limited. Traditionally, there had been only one but Aeschylus had added a second. When Sophocles added yet a third, Aeschylus followed suit. Sophocles' later plays call for four actors, as do the dramas of Euripides. Though the number of actors remained at four, this did not mean that the number of characters was also limited to four. By changing their costumes or masks the actors were able to play other roles in the same play. Indeed, not even the main character was exempted from the duty of playing other roles. The actor who played the part of Antigone, for example, took over the role of Tiresias after Antigone's death. (We have already mentioned that female roles were played by male actors, as was the case in Shakespeare's time and as is still done in the Japanese *Noh* theater.)

The use of stereotyped characters by dramatists began fairly early in Greece, just as it did in other national dramas whose development we can trace. It was paralleled by the introduction of stereotyped masks, costumes, and even a certain way of acting particular roles. Even in classical Greek tragedy we can detect the type underlying the character, but the type always takes on personal traits and becomes a definite individual marked by his fate.

In Sophocles, for example, there is not a single main character who does not show such human, individual qualities. Neither Antigone, nor Oedipus, nor Philoctetes is a mere type. But since we can usually distinguish the type behind the individual, it is helpful to examine the various types. We shall deal first with those directly concerned in the unfolding of the tragedy, and then with those lesser characters who are not directly concerned.

The "old man" is usually portrayed with a white wig, a long robe, and a staff on which he supports himself. Tiresias has the attributes of the seer—a crooked staff and a garland—in both *Antigone* and *Oedipus the King*. In *Oedipus at Colonus*, Creon, the aging king of Thebes, wears the long, decorated robe of a monarch, and carries a scepter and a sword.

The "mature man" is usually bearded and still strong, very much like the Poseidon statue of Artemision. In time of war he carries a sword and wears a short tunic with thorax (or breastplate), greaves, braces, and helmet. Odysseus and the Atridae in *Ajax* were probably dressed in this way, as were Heracles in *The Women of Trachis*, Aegisthus in *Electra*, Odys-

seus in *Philoctetes*, and Theseus in *Oedipus at Colonus*.
Oedipus himself, in *Oedipus at Colonus*, represents
this type fallen on hard times—in beggar's garb, haggard, and fatally ill.

The "thirty-or forty-year-old man" is usually the
beardless, the heroic type; as king he wears a suitably
long robe and a crown; he carries a scepter. In war-
time this type also wears a short tunic with thorax,
greaves, braces, and helmet, and he carries a sword.
Ajax and Oedipus as kings are examples of this type.
Philoctetes is one of this type in decline—sick and in
rags, he nevertheless has the bow of Heracles.

The "young man," between sixteen and twenty-
five, is usually clad in a sort of tunic and carries a
sword. Examples are: Teucer in *Ajax*, Haemon in *Antigone*, Hyllus in *The Women of Trachis*, Orestes and
Pylades in *Electra*, Neoptolemus in *Philoctetes*, and
Polynices in *Oedipus at Colonus*.

The "older woman," about fifty, wears a long robe.
As a queen, she wears a splendidly decorated dress,
with a kind of wrap over this. In addition she wears
jewelry and a crown. Eurydice in *Antigone*, Jocasta
in *Oedipus the King*, Deianira in *The Women of
Trachis*, and Clytemnestra in *Electra* are examples of
this type.

The "young lady," unmarried and in her twenties,
appears in only one Sophocles play: Electra is dressed
in a maidservant's garb and wears a mask showing
careworn features.

The "mother" also appears but once in Sophocles,
and then in the plain dress of a slave: Tecmessa in
Ajax.

The "girl," under twenty, wears a long, sleeveless,
bright-colored robe. Antigone and Ismene are such

characters. In *Antigone* they are princesses with the attributes of royalty. In *Oedipus at Colonus*, Antigone is clothed in the tattered rags of a beggar girl, while Ismene wears the garb of a wanderer with the usual wide-brimmed hat. Another example of this type is Chrysothemis in *Electra*; the role of the mysterious and beautiful—and silent— Iole in *The Women of Trachis* also conforms to this pattern.

The types drawn from the ranks of the ordinary people have been given such individuality by Sophocles that they are scarcely recognizable as types any longer. The herald in *The Women of Trachis* is an officer with military bearing; he is virile, yet discreet. The guard in *Antigone*, who reappears at one point as the messenger, is full of confidence; he is a soldier and an intelligent representative of the people. The herdman and the Corinthian messenger in *Oedipus the King* are both old men, but of totally different characters. The herdsman is somewhat timid, the messenger naively self-assured.

The servant in *Electra* who had been responsible for the upbringing of Orestes is an old man; intelligent and jolly, he is still somewhat conscious of his former position as instructor, and a little bit of a gossip. In *Philoctetes*, there is a soldier or sailor who, disguised as a shipowner, shows himself to be capable, eloquent, and intelligent. Then there are a few types who are a little less colorful, a little less convincing as individuals. Their significance as characters is exhusted once they have said their piece and left the stage. There are the messengers (soldiers or servants, for the most part) in *Ajax*, *Oedipus the King*, and *Oedipus at Colonus* and the priest in *Oedipus the King*. In all the extant plays there is but one female part drawn from the people. It is that of the nurse in *The Women of Trachis*. This is a brilliant role. She is very old; cleverer than many of the nobles, she is entrusted with the shattering news of the death of her mistress.

In Aeschylus' tragedies the hero is either the mature type (Agamemnon) or the young man (Orestes). In Sophocles' dramas, however, the picture is incomparably richer, since the types, as we have seen, are greater in number and more varied in character.

Ajax is nearest to the old man type. But Heracles, modeled on the hero in his fifties, has a definite stamp of his own. Antigone, the first female protagonist we know of, must have been a tremendous gamble: a young girl as the heroine! The ideal of heroic bravery, of the active hero, such as is incorporated in Ajax and Heracles, is transcended in Oedipus as king, for he is not only courageous but also has great intellectual stature and is a ruling monarch. Electra as a heroine is so complex a figure that she can be explained only in conjunction with Orestes.

Philoctetes, like some figures in Euripides' tragedies, represents the hero in decline. Still in his thirties, he is already haggard. True, he still bears the bow of Heracles and carries himself as a hero. The decline shown in Philoctetes is even greater in Oedipus, fallen in *Oedipus at Colonus* from his former glory. Though scarcely fifty, he looks upon himself as an old man, a living corpse, and staggers around on the arm of his daughter. But though he is far removed from his former glory, his spirit remains unbroken; his conduct is that of a great hero.

How much of this was cult or ritual? The traditional type could be distinguished behind the character, but mask, costume, and theatrical appearance in

general combined to show the character of great individuals, as did the quality of the acting.

What the mask hid or could not express was conveyed by a gesture, an actor's gait or movement. This
was intended to appear spontaneous, even though it
was carefully rehearsed. We can only imagine the
mimic expression from the words, and we can only get
a vague idea of the acting from pictorial art, where the
expression shown is not only motionless but also
adapted to the overall composition of the picture.

Sophocles' text leaves no doubt that excitement was
conveyed spontaneously by actions and gestures and
that the actor had to concentrate on achieving this
excitement by means of his imagination. Sudden fear,
growing anxiety, the change from doubt to certainty,
and outbreak of joy, the plunging to the depths of
despair, raging anger, horror and lamentation—all this
had to be acted out convincingly. The goal every
dramatist aimed at was excitement. This was a theater
of passion.

It has already been pointed out that there were conventional gestures of lamentation and joy. In the
dramatic situations of Sophocles' dramas, emotional
gestures may have been ritualized, but starting from
the conventionally automatic the actor was able to
direct his own emotions into the special situation of
the character being depicted. The gesture developed
from the conventional into the particular and individual. Since no stage directions were written in the text,
we can only determine how things were by looking
closely at the text itself. We shall accordingly examine
the types of spoken verses in order to ascertain just
how the actor must have played his particular role.

The mode of expression of tragedy was the dialogue, which consisted of speech and counterspeech. We shall deal first of all with the speech. In Sophocles' plays this is never a mere showpiece tirade, never rhetoric for rhetoric's sake. On the one occasion where we do find more rhetoric (in the report of Orestes' "death" in *Electra*), the speaker is being deliberately deceptive. The rhetorical is, however, an important element in tragedy and is usually included in the drama as a report (by a messenger, for example), declaration, accusation, or defense. The report has a definite structure, invariably beginning, in the case of Sophocles, with the expression of the emotion or mood of the messenger. What he says is "pathetic" in the true sense of the word, for he reports not so much as if he has merely witnessed everything, but as if he has actually experienced it. And when he has given his account, he concludes by repeating both the emotion and the report in the form of a reflection. This reflection, also pathetic in tone, requires a response.

Declarations are constructed in a similar way. An edict will be given in the language of the law, as an expression of a dominant will. The speaker then deals with the reasons behind, and the consequences of, the edict. He spares himself no effort, turns from one person to another commandingly or threateningly, and works himself up into such a passion that a reaction must ensue, whether it be only a soft murmuring from the chorus or an embarrassed silence.

The majority of the longer speeches are written in the style of parliamentary debate or legal process. Arguments are introduced and directed toward the rational proof of a thesis with which the speaker confronts both the characters on the stage and the audience. Such speeches are always directed toward the counterspeech. They are dialectic, so that we find the forensic speech of the constitutional state pitted against the will of the people as it emerges in a democracy. The speeches often tend toward the theoretical and touch upon the political, the moral, the philosophic or the theological. Usually these addresses have gnomic endings, pithy summarizing sentences.

Sophocles never allows a dramatic incident to stand in total isolation. By virtue of its dialectic interpretation, every single aspect of the plot, every event, is very much a part of the world in which the characters live, whether it be the world represented on the stage or the contemporary world of the audience—for the dramatist was always conscious of writing for his time. Why, after all, should a play be performed unless it bore some relevance to the lives of the people watching it?

Whenever the chorus gave its opinion after a great speech or counterspeech (it did so with what we would consider uncomfortable directness), and summed up by saying that both sides had argued well, it was merely reflecting that objectivity which Sophocles considered essential to any dramatist. If the hero's opponents were not supplied with telling counterarguments which made sense to his partners on the stage, the chorus, and the audience, then the hero's arguments, too, would be considered worthless and without weight.

As was true in Aeschylus' dramas, the speech and counterspeech in Sophocles' tragedies were developed by logical steps until two equally justified views or attitudes are seen to be quite irreconcilably opposed. At such a point the tragic bind is revealed as a condition of human existence. The hero then stands before a choice which will plunge him into guilt no matter what his decision. It is an essential characteristic of the hero that he stands by his decision, even though he may be deserted or even damned by the gods.

By means of dramatic dialogue the dialectic shatters the contrasts and drives them to extremes. The way of doing this is inherent in the nature of the dialogue. Sophocles uses this method as one possibility of expressing a discussion between two—and in the later dramas, three—persons in a manner befitting the compelling truth of the situation and characters.

The long speeches and counterspeeches are often summarized in shorter sections of about ten lines each. But these sections can also stand alone in opposition to one another and without any imposing speeches preceding them. They usually signify that time is pressing. At other times, speeches may be no more than two-line units which continue for considerable periods, sometimes as a climax to more lengthy sections, sometimes as independent units. The dialogue is not always dialectical in such passages. The dramatist uses them to present information dramatically, as one character slowly extorts from the other that which the others on stage (and the audience) must know. Such dialogue is particularly well suited to an interrogation which sometimes takes on the character of a cross-examination.

In this scheme the dialogue is sometimes reduced to a single line immediately followed by a one-line rejoinder (*stichomythía*). This adds to the tension, and has a sharpening and heightening effect. A further possibility within this stylistic scheme is to break up the lines into mere phrases or even single words, which strike home like arrows.

A sharp observer of human nature, Sophocles uses

dialogue to characterize the speaker. Obviously, the servant speaks differently from his master, and this is expressed stylistically by even including slang expressions. Significantly, a servant might even express sounder views than his more stubborn or narrow-minded master (the guard in the *Antigone* is such an example). The mood of the text indicates the correct way of portraying the role.

The way in which the voices of Oedipus, Jocasta, and a man of the people are played off one against the other is masterly! And how magnificently and suddenly the voice of the divine rings out as Heracles speaks from the tops of the rocks and resolves the acute tragic bind between the heroically tragic Philoctetes and the simple and honest young Neoptolemus! What a contrast there is between the harsh, blind beggar Oedipus and the candid, unostentatious regality of Theseus! We are offered a spectrum of human possibilities in the state, in society, or in the family.

In none of the extant plays are there any love scenes. True, there are lovers, but they do not speak to one another of their love. At most they might make an appeal to an uncooperative partner concerning a matter other than love, and even in such cases it is a wife or mother, rather than a lover, who makes the appeal. It seems as if there were no place for the intimate on the stage. The chorus might sing of Eros' power, but the hero shows no sign of *éros* and scarcely ever speaks of it. The great scenes which Sophocles wrote for lovers—Haemon's fruitless intervention on behalf of his intended bride, Antigone, and Deianira's hapless struggle for the heart of her husband (*The Women of Trachis*)—take place without one of the lovers on stage.

The language rises to great heights when it shows

the same people in different situations. There is in Sophoclean tragedy none of the self-destruction which drives Shakespeare's heroes to the brink of ruin and even further. Neither is there any of the dissolution of the personality to the point of interchangeability such as we find in some modern dramatists. But within the frame of human existence his tragedy jerks the character out of his self-confidence and makes him realize that in extreme situations the human being is powerless.

Whoever compares Oedipus' speeches at the beginning of the drama with those at the end without reading what comes between will find it impossible to believe that this is the same person speaking. But whoever looks at the tragedy as a whole—remembering the hero as he appeared at the beginning—will notice that the possibilities of the end were already present in the very first speeches. Once, right at the beginning, Oedipus speaks of the sleepless nights of care. In other words, he is capable as a human being and a hero of feeling the incomprehensible (in this case the plague afflicting the city) and seeing the darkness which engulfs all existence. The great knower will blind himself because he has come up against the limits of this knowledge. The possibility of the outcome is inserted into the opening of the play like a thorn in the flesh whose nagging presence becomes increasingly obvious. It is suggested in the opening scenes and, through language, is quietly developed and grows from strength to strength in each speech the hero makes.

It is not only the change in the hero's self-confidence which is expressed by means of language. The stages marked by the deeds of the hero are also given expression in the text. For example, the rage and indignation which enable Antigone to act as she does are matched by the furious tone of her dialogue. Immediately after the deed, her speech reflects in its clarity and calm the almost superhuman determination of the perfect heroine, only to decline finally into mortal fear in the face of the reality of death.

Sophocles not only separates determination and passing mood, the rational and the irrational emotion and reason in his portrayal of man, but also frequently allows them to merge one into the other. Even where pure reason is emphasized, language is dependent on the state the person is in as well as on the character of this person. But the treatment makes it plain that just as one particular and momentary state cannot represent the true essence of a person, neither can a person's range of thinking be determined simply by one mood. When stressing a thought, the actor must always remain aware of the emotional state to which the situation is driving the character, so that at any time (as in a sudden recognition of the tragic bind he is in) the emotion can effectively erupt out of his dialectic. An example of this is Oedipus' "O city, city!"

T. S. Eliot was quite right to call the text which Sophocles put into the actors' hands a kind of "shorthand." There is, as it were, a perspective to the words: they always reveal something which cannot actually be expressed by words, but which can be depicted by an action, a gesture, by the movement or posture of the actor. The meaning behind the words, between the lines, is *shown* by the actor. Such meaning can be gathered from countless apparently insignificant turns of phrase, from pauses, from the sound of the words and the tempo of the verse. The possibilities of the dialogue are fulfilled only upon being completed by acting. Without it the poet would not have been able to complete his text. In a sense, the poet, who was his own director, directed the play in his imagination while writing it.

Nonetheless we should not forget that language was still primarily verse, rhythm, sound—in a word, it was poetry. The process followed in the combination of form and content is mysterious, but the results are undisputed. If language and art had not been combined perfectly through the genius of Sophocles, these tragedies would hardly have survived for twenty-four hundred years. Through art, truth achieves the form in which the two are welded into a lasting unity. The form is both developed and perpetuated by its content.

As long as the dramatist was writing tragedies for the theater, he was faced with a system which he could not disregard. The arrangement of the action taking place was as fixed as the possibilities of the dialogue—verse, speech, speech and counterspeech, *stichomythía*. Then there was the whole complex matter of the chorus, a sort of erratic block from another age, which had to be fitted into the new form. The combination of the chorus and dialogue put into action resulted in "theater."

The disparateness of the component parts of early tragedy is still obvious in the later dramas. But a poet like Sophocles made it his business, as it were, to reinvent the combination and not leave it to historical accident to determine the form for him. He allowed the combination to develop out of the inner necessity of the play in question. The chorus was coordinated with the dialogue and each in turn was adjusted to the presentation. Hence situations had to be invented in which the chorus seems to flow naturally out of the dialogue, always as reflection or as a spontaneous emotional response. In other cases the dialogue seems to be prefigured by the chorus.

Sometimes the dialogue could actually develop out of a choral passage, but such a transition then invariably presented a major problem combining the various formal details. The solution to this problem (from Aeschylus on) lay in antiphony. Antiphonal song was sung (and danced) by the chorus with one or two (sometimes three) soloists. It always has an instrumental accompaniment, and is often interrupted by spoken dialogue. The resulting combination is as artistically constructed as the choral songs themselves (with strophe, antistrophe and other proportionally arranged refinements). The chorus and soloists do not sing in unison, so that the essential quality of dialogue is preserved. The music, however, suggests that something in the dialogue has changed and shows a tendency towards the choral.

Sophocles, throughout his career, brought the art of antiphony to ever greater degrees of perfection. Only in the work of a Mozart or Verdi do we find a comparable synthesis of lyric flow and dramatic tension. The song always springs directly from the dialogue and it is impelled toward its climax. It is, in fact, a continuation of the dialogue through other means.

It usually begins when the dialectic exchange has concluded and the characters are overcome by emotion. The instruments strike up, the actor becomes a singer and the chorus responds with song. Rhythm and song (*mélos*) seek to attain greater expression through antiphonal song. Grief is poured out in a loud lament, and joy is expressed in rapturous hymns.

When the action reaches an impasse, fear, confusion, or supplication can unleash the antiphonal song which might rise to a state of highest ecstasy, or break out into insane terror, before gradually subsiding into a more composed lamentation. But sometimes it takes only a spoken exchange recalling the terrible truth to unleash new cries of anguish, which, in their turn, are taken up by music and song in one unified rhythmic and strophic movement.

Just as, in moments of silence, a simple action can sometimes express the deepest tragedy, so, too, does music express in sound that which cannot be expressed in any other way. Art makes it possible to combine the choral song and the dialogue into a single entity which is part of a final composite form. Traditional theatrical form is thereby raised to a higher plane, for this combination is now seen from the point of view of the whole play, as part of a greater and planned unity.

Through the form, the world represented on the stage comes to represent the whole world. Reason (*lógos*) is given expression primarily in the dialogue; emotion in the choral song. But there are in each possibilities for transition to or reflection of the other. Together with the action on the stage, a kind of animated sculpture, these means of expression combine to form a view of life.

It is a tragic view of life. Each scene is simply one dimension of the whole of existence. The hero embodies human nature and reason (*physis* and *lógos*) in an unusual human situation. Whether, as with Oedipus, it is the spirit which raises him above all others, or whether, as with Antigone, it is love (*philía*—not sexual love) which is the distinguishing feature, or whether as with Heracles, it is the power of a great spirit, these heroes invariably are caught in extreme situations which cause them to founder.

It lies in the nature of tragedy, as we have said, to make man conscious of the possibility of foundering. The gods strike. They are beyond good and evil, and they make no distinction between right and wrong.

In foundering, in meeting his end, the tragic hero pits himself against both man and the gods. In the certain knowledge of his innocence he preserves his human dignity, even though he is doomed to death, reduced to rags, to a mere nothing.

At the end of his long life, Sophocles, one of the greatest poets of all time, allowed a ray of hope to fall on the tragic picture of human existence. Posterity offers the tragic hero who is destroyed by the world, or destroyed while the world looks on, the reward of immortality for his sufferings. The gods, too, are part of the drama, and hence we see a light from another world shedding its light around the dying Oedipus.

PLAYS

Ajax

The Background

In the tenth year of the Trojan War an argument flared up among the leaders of the Greeks as to who should have the famous weapons of Achilles now that he was dead. Ajax, second only to Achilles in martial prowess, laid claim to them. But Agamemnon and his brother Menelaus, the sons of Atreus, contrived to have them given to their friend Odysseus.

For Ajax this is a monstrous insult. His prestige in the army and his fame throughout the world are in jeopardy. He retires to his tent and plots revenge. In the night before the action of the play begins, he rises and, with sword in hand, sets off to confront Agamemnon, Menelaus, and Odysseus in their tents. But the goddess Athena intervenes and protects the unsuspecting Greeks from Ajax's wrath by afflicting him with an "illness," making him temporarily insane. Ajax mistakes a herd of cattle for the Greeks and, turning upon them in great rage, slaughters a large number of them. He returns to his tent with the bloody carcasses. One hapless creature he drives before him, imagining that this beast is Odysseus and intending to torture it to death.

The Prologue

As dawn breaks, Odysseus, who has heard news of these incredible events, appears before Ajax's tent to see what has been going on. With him is Athena, who remains invisible but addresses him and explains the night's events. After calling to Ajax, she advises the apprehensive Odysseus to stand quietly by and observe: Is it not the sweetest laughter to laugh at your enemies' downfall?

Ajax, covered with gore from the cattle, comes out from his tent. Still in his fit of madness, he exults triumphantly over his act of revenge. Odysseus is horrified and reflects: If the gods can deal like this with such a man, what then are we all, we humans? Nothing but dim shapes—weightless shadows.

Scenes Concerning the Death of Ajax

Ajax's suicide is part of the myth about him, but Sophocles gives it his own interpretation. The Chorus, consisting of soldiers from Ajax's army, enters the scene. Tecmessa, a princess taken prisoner during the war, now a slave and concubine to Ajax and mother of his beloved son, rushes out of the tent toward the soldiers. Breathlessly she tells them what has happened and goes on to describe the hero's dreadful state of mind now that he has returned to sanity and to the full realization of his actions. Never has she seen him in such pain, never has she heard such terrible cries of agony from a man who normally conceals all pain and grief. And now he sits amid his bloody kill, alternately brooding over his deeds and lamenting them.

The antiphony begins. We hear Ajax's lamentations issuing from the tent. He calls for his son and for Teucer, his half brother, who should long ago have returned from an expedition. The *eccýclema* is wheeled out, Tecmessa pulls back the tent flaps and the terrible spectacle is revealed in all its horror. Anguished words pour out of the grief-stricken hero: Overwhelmed by shame, he yearns to die. Then, drained of emotion, he falls silent. The music comes to an end. The dialogue starts. The gods have stricken him; they are on his enemies' side. What can he do to save his honor and be able one day to look his father in the eyes again?

He weighs three possibilities. The first two he quickly rejects: he can neither return home nor throw himself into the battle wilfully seeking death. The third and most difficult choice is suicide. To take his sword and plunge it into his breast is no simple matter, for the world is both dear and hateful to him. To leave what is dear without having hunted down and defeated that which is hateful is his tragic fate: "To nobly live or nobly die?" That is the question. To live with such unbearable shame in such an intolerable world is impossible. But can he find an honorable death? Tecmessa throws herself at his feet and his little son is brought before him. He takes him in his arms and expresses the hope that his son will fare better at the hands of the fates than he did. Then, thrusting

Tecmessa and the child from him, he bids them: "Close up the tent. No more lamenting!"

The *eccýclema* is wheeled off, and the Chorus sings in praise of the distant fatherland. Ajax appears with Tecmessa, his sword in his hand. Strangely enough he now seems to have changed his mind, and he describes apparently, how his iron resolve has weakened. In future he will give way before the gods and submit to the Atridae—Agamemnon and Menelaus. With this, he bids Tecmessa go and pray for him, and he asks the Chorus to report everything to Teucer. He goes down to the shore "to cleanse his stains" and bury his sword, this most "hateful of weapons."

This celebrated speech of deception has three purposes. First, it is designed to allow Ajax to die alone; nobody is to interfere, nobody is to hear his last lament. That he succeeds in this ploy is demonstrated by the Chorus, which now bursts into joyful song at this "salvation." Second, it is a blow at his enemies. They will exult at his submission, but then be thunderstruck, when they learn of his deeds. In this way, the army will be able to see who the true criminals are. Third, this scene is an experiment for both Ajax himself and the audience. He seems to be saying: "Let us assume that a man like me heeds the advice of the others and resolves to live. What would happen then? He would be accepting the injustice of this world, a world without truth or friendship." The experiment is the final act: his recognition that he cannot submit, and that he must act. The audience recognizes the dignity of his death, and so he goes down to the sea.

At this point there is an interlude. A messenger arrives and announces an oracle. Ajax shall be saved if he survives the day—this is the will of Athena. Tecmessa and the Chorus hurry off after him.

With the tent removed from the scene, the grove and the sea are visible below. Climbing the steps behind the stage, Ajax carefully fixes his sword so that he can fall upon it. His last monologue is full of the deepest pathos. He flings a last curse at his hated enemies and bestows a last greeting on his dear friends. Ajax loves the life he is now about to deprive himself of, but he can neither change nor accept what the gods have ordained. Deserted by the gods, but unafraid of them, he washes the stain from his character by destroying that which bears the stain: his life. His last action insures fame and the respect of the just hereafter.

The rest is lament and ritual. Tecmessa finds the corpse. A dummy with the sword sticking out from the breast is brought onto the scene on a bier. Teucer arrives and the child is brought in to pay his last respects to his father.

The Epilogue

Menelaus enters in a towering rage and tries to prevent the burial. Teucer refuses to obey his command and the Chorus stands firmly behind him. When Menelaus brings his brother to the scene, the latter's speeches abusing the dead hero are cut short by Odysseus, who persuades Agamemnon not to desecrate the dead man. He convinces him that his prestige in the Greek army will rise if he honors that which is noble in his enemy. Teucer thanks Odysseus, but does not

permit him to take part in the burial. In solemn procession the body is borne from the stage.

The three great scenes leading Ajax into the isolation of death represent the demonstration and protest
of a great individual against the world in which man
acts as he does and is ruled over by the gods. Though
this situation has particular relevance for us today, it is
based on mythological presuppositions which make
for difficulties. For the Athenians it was quite clear
that Ajax had first claim to the weapons since he was
second only to Achilles in martial prowess. The illness
inflicted upon him by the gods (in fact all of Athena's
actions and speeches) was bound up with the Greek
notion of the squabbling gods. The argument over the
burial reflects the love for disputation current in
Sophocles' time. It is difficult therefore to arouse a
modern audience's interest unless cuts are made.

Antigone

The Background

In order to escape disastrous consequences prophesied to them, Oedipus' sons resolved to share the sov-
ereignty of Thebes: each was to occupy the throne
for one year. But Eteocles, who had ascended to the
throne first by virtue of his seniority, refused to give
up his authority to his brother Polynices, as had been
arranged. Polynices, who had meanwhile married the
princess of Argos, enlisted the aid of six princes and
marched on Thebes. Two days prior to the action of
the play, the two brothers had met in decisive combat
before the gates of Thebes, and each had inflicted
mortal wounds on the other. The following night, the
attacking army withdrew and during the next day and
night the city celebrated its victory and the coming of
peace. Creon, Oedipus' brother-in-law, has seized
power and moved into the palace with his family.
Oedipus' daughters, Antigone and Ismene, continue to
live in the palace.

The Edict

Early in the morning the side door leading to the women's quarters is pushed open and Antigone rushes out, pulling her sister after her. She is highly incensed, and Ismene is terrified. Inside the palace they were unable to speak and now Antigone tells her sister the terrible news. Creon has gone into the city to proclaim that the body of the treacherous Polynices is not to be given proper burial. Instead it is to be left to be devoured by the birds and dogs. Whoever disobeys this edict shall be stoned to death. Ismene is as horrified at this news as her sister, but asks what they—weak women—can do about it. But though her sister fears to challenge Creon, Antigone is sure of her own actions: she will do alone what the gods' sacred commands require. What worse than death can happen to her?

Ismene begs her sister to be careful and at least act secretly. But Antigone sees no reason to hide what she considers to be a perfectly just and respectable act. "I shall hate you, if you do not shout it to all the world," she announces before running off to the battlefield, where her brother's body lies.

We hear joyful, bacchantic music and the Chorus enters. It is the council of elders convened by Creon to represent the people. However, he has not summoned them to hear their advice, but to receive his orders, for the edict has already been proclaimed. The picture of the reeling elders, still intoxicated from the peace celebration, cavorting around is in direct and ironic contrast to the somber prologue.

Their dance is suddenly interrupted by the sound of marching and the clash of weapons. Creon enters the scene at the head of his bodyguard and takes up position in front of the great palace gate on the raised platform. He uses the proclamation of his first action as head of state as an announcement of policy. He demands obedience and solidarity.

Whoever is not unequivocally for the tyrant will be looked upon as a traitor. The deed Antigone is planning accordingly takes on even greater significance: She is the only one who will dare to challenge this show of authoritarian terror by defying the decree to leave Polynices unburied.

An armed guard slinks in from the same side on which Antigone had made her exit. No longer young, he is aware of what he can expect by way of thanks for the announcement he has to make. He is so frightened that it requires threats of force to make him divulge that someone has buried the corpse and escaped undetected. Creon is furious and accuses the guard of having slept. We now learn the true reason for the edict. It was simply a means of bringing Creon's enemies out into the open so that he could liquidate them. He sends the guard off with a threat: He will be tortured unless the guilty person is brought before Creon.

Then there is silence. The Chorus says not a word. Only the guard dares to speak up, pointing out that he would scarcely have brought the message if he had had anything to do with the deed. Mad with rage, Creon leaves him standing there and strides off into the palace; shaking his head, the guard exits. The Chorus chants the famous song that begins: "Many are the wonders but nothing more wonderful than man." It is a hymn to the human spirit and human power.

The Arrest

The guard returns with Antigone in fetters. He is glad to have avoided punishment even though he regrets getting friends into trouble. The Chorus is dismayed; Creon, who now reenters, is very much surprised. He immediately assigns political motivations to Antigone's act. If his enemies had wanted a symbol for the rebellion, who could be more appropriate than the heir to the throne?

Antigone is completely changed. No longer the frenzied girl, she is a cool, realistic mistress of the situation. She admits the deed and the fact that she contravened the edict, but she argues that she acted according to the divine justice of the unwritten law.

Curbing his rage, Creon condescends to her from his position of power, his tone being one that might be used with a slave. He knows how he can wound her, and he commands Ismene to be brought before him. We all know, of course, that Ismene is innocent. But the arrow hits its mark and Antigone reacts: "Do you want more than my arrest and death?" She taunts him, hoping that he will have her executed on the spot. Pointing to all present (the Chorus, representatives of the people) she mockingly notes that they would agree with her if only their tongues were not tied by fear. She knows the political significance of her deed, and she is aware that Creon is vulnerable because he is unsure of his grasp on power.

He opens the dialogue with two arguments, pointing out that Antigone stands alone and that she has dishonored her one brother, the defender of Thebes, by burying her other brother, a traitor to Thebes. To the first point Antigone says only that the others are simply too cowardly to give her open support. To the second point she says that though in life "I may have no right to side with one or another; in death other laws prevail." Once dead Polynices is simply her brother. Creon answers that: "Not even in death does an enemy become a friend." Antigone's reply to this is famous: "Not to hate was I born, but to love."

Much has been written about this statement, and scholars have disagreed on its general significance. Some are of the opinion that Antigone simply wanted to express that, as a sister, she was born to love her brother. She is therefore defending the bond of kinship. But the fact that Creon makes no reply to this statement suggests that Sophocles wished to endow this last word of the dialogue with a degree of finality. Antigone is defending the bond of kinship against arbitrary political decision. She herself has called it an *unwritten law*. What is it that is mightier than death itself—hate or love? This is the essential question around which everything that follows will turn.

With the death of those dear to him, Creon will come to realize which of the two is more powerful. That which Antigone calls love (*philía*, not *eros*) encompasses a realm which excludes power, the state and politics. Death itself is a sign that there is a limit to earthly power. After a short silence, Creon continues: "Then go down there, if you must love, and love the dead." The dialogue ends abruptly with the assertion: "No woman rules me while I live."

Armed soldiers enter with a tearful and distraught Ismene. Creon drops all pretense: "These vipers have I had in my house. I did not notice that all along I have been sheltering two traitors." He clearly still looks upon Antigone's deed as an act against the throne, the signal for rebellion. "Confess," he bellows at Ismene. And to everyone's surprise she does indeed confess her complicity. She is obviously panic-stricken. She knows she is about to lose all that remains to her. If her sister must die, why should she live? She accordingly stands by her sister, unwittingly adding fuel to Creon's fire. Antigone, who earlier tried to hasten her own death in order to save her sister, must now brusquely repudiate Ismene, if she is to succeed in her purpose.

It is again *philía* that motivates Antigone, and this time the one she loves, Ismene, is still alive. Only once does Antigone answer her sister's reproach that she does her injury, and then she does so with strange ambiguity: "I also suffer, when I laugh at you." Ismene once again twists the dialectic one spiral higher (after Antigone has convinced everyone that she had refused to be implicated in the burial) by raising the subject of Haemon, Creon's son and Antigone's future husband. To this Creon cynically remarks: "There are enough other wives for his plow."

Ismene replies that it is not this that matters, but what binds a man to his wife. The Chorus attempts to intervene, but Creon quickly gives the command to take the women inside. Antigone's execution is to be prepared. A bridge to the next scene is provided by a choral lament construing Antigone's fate as the will of the gods.

The Intervention

Haemon enters in the mask and costume of the young man. He is clearly troubled. Antigone's youth is reflected in the youth of her lover. He has just come

from the city, where the rumor of her death sentence
has aroused the people. Creon appeals to his son's loyalty and insists that order in the state entails obedience
to the laws and toward those who formulate them.
The greatest of evils is anarchy; the citizen's foremost
duty is obedience to the ruler.

Haemon, knowing his father, is aware that only political arguments impress him. He warns Creon that
the polis does not stand behind him in this matter and
advises him to be very careful. Creon's answer to this
is characteristic: is the town to tell him how to rule?
Haemon's rejoinder points to the political meaning of
the play: one man's arbitrary rule will work in deserts
only. At this Creon flies into a rage. Then, when
Haemon states that he, too, will die if Antigone dies,
Creon tells him venomously that Antigone will be executed before his eyes. Enraged at his father's malice,
Haemon rushes off.

Farewell to Life

We now see how Creon covers up his growing uncertainty through harsh and erratic measures. True, he
is persuaded by the Chorus to spare Ismene's life, but
he decides on the cruelest of fates for Antigone. She is
to be immured alive in a cave.

Now begins one of the most tragic of scenes. Antigone is brought from the palace by the guards. Her
head is shaved and she is wearing the garb normally
reserved for criminals. Her arms are locked behind her
back and tied to a pole. The Chorus gives vent to its
horror and sorrow.

The music starts up and the antiphony begins.

There is another section of dialogue and then a return to antiphony. Then there is again a dialectic exchange which rises to a climax. With death so close, Antigone is overcome by despair. No tragic hero goes willingly to death. What kind of heroine is she? Is she super-human or fanatical enough to leave this life for an idea or a belief? She is neither a Christian martyr nor a heroine for a political cause. She is a girl who, in he-roic indignation, has dared a bold deed and is now faced with monstrous consequences. Her ecstatic la-ment is cruelly transformed into a recognition of her earthly fate. The Chorus, which joined in her lament, calls her the equal of the gods.

But Antigone interprets these words as mockery. If she were the equal of the gods she would hardly have to die! Where are her loved ones now? Is she not alone and deserted by both the gods and man? Her deed was also for the polis, and the polis has also de-serted her.

The prudent Chorus tries to wash their hands of what is happening: "You plunged from the highest peak of daring and now you face the law. Piety is fine, but might is might. One must not act against it. Your rebellion has brought you down." And with these words the heroine is repudiated by the people.

Creon rushes in from the palace and asks why there is so much delay in carrying out his orders. Antigone is still able to exert an influence over the people by virtue of the sympathy they feel for her, and almost as if Creon were not present, she once again describes the motives behind her act. Her love for her father, mother and brother was the prime cause; she will meet them again in the next world and be welcomed by them.

And now come those ominous lines which Goethe once hoped would be proved spurious, and which scholars still dispute today. Antigone maintains that she would not have done it for a husband or for children, and we may readily accept that this is true, for she had experienced neither marriage nor motherhood. But the reasoning which follows is almost ludicrous: it is possible, she says, to replace a husband or even children, but totally impossible to replace a brother once one's parents are dead!

Perhaps it was Sophocles' intention to have Antigone speak in this "rational" way in order to show that she was still in possession of her faculties. Perhaps he wanted to express the purity of her love—*philía* as opposed to *eros*. But we may have to accept these lines as unexplainable. They are, after all, no more than a transition to an observation of considerably deeper significance: If it was right what I have done, why then am I forsaken by the gods and by men? How can I, so ill-fated, look up to the gods and ask for their help? They have forsaken me. If I only knew in what I failed!

Antigone is not guilty, and she does not feel so. Nor does Sophocles think her guilty. To be deserted by the gods is man's lot in tragedy; it is part of the human condition. Yet at this stage of his career, Sophocles still believes that an audience will recognize the injustice and perceive that the heroine's actions were right and proper. He accordingly has Antigone awaken from her musings. She points to the truly guilty, namely Creon and the Chorus, and says: But if it is the others who are wrong, I wish them no greater punishment than what they do to me with their power.

As Creon and the Chorus begin to move off with

her executioners, Antigone puts together in a few fiery lines of verse an indictment not only of her own world but also of Sophocles' own time and of ours, too. Her indictment damns both those in power and those who submit to this power.

The effect is inspiring. Antigone, the true queen by virtue of birth, is dragged off in fetters like some notorius criminal. The audience must ask itself whether it, too, would allow such things to happen.

The Seer's Curse

After the Chorus has conjured up mythical parallels, Tiresias, the blind seer, is led in by a young lad. He bears the crooked staff of a seer and is represented as extremely old. In all, it is an archetypal image evoking awe. Yet he, too, bears a message of current relevance, one with political ramifications. This holy man had sanctioned Creon's accession to the throne. But the latter did not consult Tiresias when he issued the edict, and now the seer has come in fulfillment of his official duty. The situation in Thebes has become tense and there are forebodings of evil. The altars are sullied by the leavings of the birds and the dogs who had feasted on Polynices' corpse. There are ominous murmurings from the people. The scene begins, then, where the scene between Haemon and Creon left off. Tiresias directs his appeal not to fear but to reason.

By now Creon has taken leave of his senses, and we hear the rantings of a man with an acute persecution complex. Clearly the seer must have been bribed by rebels; indeed, they all (i.e., the Chorus) have betrayed him. But not even Zeus himself will force him to bury Polynices with the proper rites. Finally the seer loses patience with Creon, and resorts to prophecy. His words and tone make the clay colossus waver:

> Soon wailing will echo through your house,
> And all the *poleis* will rise up against your own,
> Where birds and dogs pay the last respects to the
> dead
> And where the stench of corpses pollutes the air.

As Creon's determination begins to fail, the Chorus, which now dares to speak, exhorts him to bury the corpse quickly and to free Antigone from the cave in which she has been immured.

The Catastrophe

When Creon hurries off with his bodyguard, the Chorus, as it had done on its initial appearance, introduces an unconsciously ironic tone into the proceedings: everything will now be fine; Antigone and Haemon will now return in triumph; Tiresias will give his blessing to the wedding of Oedipus' daughter and Creon's son, and both will now rule over the polis. However, this is nothing but the same senile enthusiasm which caused the Chorus to sing and dance earlier in the play—bacchantically, of course, for the cult of Dionysus had its principal center in Thebes.

The messenger comes running in with sad tidings for those now gathered so joyfully together. He is the same man we met earlier as the guard; in other words, he is the representative of the common folk. His lamentations are so loud that Eurydice, Creon's wife, who is inside the palace, comes hurrying out to find out what has gone wrong. Only Shakespeare could have invented horrors comparable to those we now learn of: on opening the cave Creon and his guard had found Haemon mourning at the feet of Antigone, who had hanged herself. At the sight of his father, Haemon spat in his face and threw himself on his sword.

Without a word, Eurydice flees into the women's quarters in the palace. There is a painful silence and then the messenger is ordered to find out what is wrong. He goes in search of Eurydice, and soon there is a sound of wailing. A horrible procession then enters the scene. Creon is carrying his son's body in his arms; he is grief-stricken and loudly curses himself. The messenger reenters, announcing that the queen, too, is dead. The central doors of the palace open and the *eccýclema* is rolled out bearing the corpse of Eurydice. Creon sets down his son's corpse and shrieks in anguish at the havoc he has wreaked. Ripping his robes open, he begs to be killed. And then the piteous admission from the once-overbearing tyrant: "I am no more than nothing now."

Haemon's body is laid on the *eccýclema* near his mother's. Creon throws himself across them. Slowly the grievous sight fades into the darkness. The words of those withdrawing exhort the audience: know thyself.

It is not simply the figure of the heroine, Sophocles' most personal creation and one which lives on into posterity, that has ensured for this play its great popularity. The world depicted on the stage is also an accurate reflection of our own world. Old and young, men and women, the rulers and the people—all combine in a configuration in whose center the heroine rises into the kind of extreme human situation through which the tragic hero achieves immortality.

The tragedy's warning to the great statesman Pericles (his title was *strategós*, and this is Antigone's designation for Creon) is still valid today. It is not (as Hegel thought) the conflict between the good of the state and love for the family as two ideas of equal importance that is so relevant. The essential moral is in the warning to those in power not to transgress those unwritten rules that set limits to political action. The play is an apologia for the power of *philía*, which is perhaps best translated as "loving-kindness."

Finally, something should be said about the admirable structure of this drama, the very epitome of the classical simplicity and greatness which the German historian Winckelmann found characteristic of the Greeks. The raging course of the opening scene is mirrored in the manic pathos of the final scene. The latent import of Creon's speech from the throne is brought out in the scene in which Haemon intervenes, and it is given striking expression in the Tiresias scene. Sophocles' dramatic technique is extreme concentration. The climax of the play, Antigone's farewell, is just over two-thirds the way through. The dramatist links it with the final section by means of the Haemon scene which precedes it.

The Women of Trachis

The Background

The source is the Heracles-Deianira myth. Heracles, son of Alcmene and Zeus (see the many Amphitryon plays: Kleist, Giraudoux *et al.*) is, however, not the glorious Homeric hero. He is not a prince and ruler; his weapon is the club, his exploits are the labors of a man paid for his services. He is a hero worshipped by the common people. Possessed of enormous strength, he is a man much given to food and drink—a fighter and a cantankerous fellow. And yet it would be an exaggeration to say that he is all brawn and no brain. His exploits serve civilization by ridding the world of monsters, evil beasts, and criminals.

But the man who pits himself against monsters would, according to the Greeks, have to be a bit of a monster himself. Again and again the gods punish Heracles for his misdeeds, and again and again he compensates for these misdeeds by the services he performs. When the action of the play starts, Heracles, his wife (Deianira), and their children have sought refuge in Trachis. Considerable time has passed since he wrested the beautiful princess from the river god who had wooed her in the strange shape of a human with an ox's head. They have grown-up sons, and Heracles is no longer a young man.

As so often happened in the past, he has gone off on his travels. But this time there is a difference. According to an oracle, he had learned that he would at last find an end to his troubles if he could survive one final adventure on Euboea. Heracles had immediately set off, pausing only to entrust Deianira with a tablet containing his last will and testament. Fifteen months have passed and no news of him has reached Trachis.

Deianira

In the opening scene Deianira confides her worst fears concerning Heracles to the aged nurse. Her mask betrays the strain of many sleepless nights. At this point her son Hyllus returns from the city. He has heard that Heracles is on Euboea. Deianira's joy at the news that Heracles is still alive is coupled with fear as he remembers the oracle's prophecy about Euboea. She urges her son to go in search of his father, and Hyllus sets off forthwith. The Chorus enters. It consists of Deianira's young companions, and these girls sing of the lonely lady's sad longing.

No less than four messengers now arrive bearing news of the hero's impending arrival. First comes a shepherd who says that Heracles' herald has brought good news. But Deianira is disturbed by the delay in the appearance of the herald himself. When he finally enters, it is at the head of a procession of women, in whose midst is a beautiful, young girl. Deianira loses all hope as she listens to Heracles' message, and she stares coldly at her new rival. She feels threatened, even as the herald assures her that he has no knowledge of the identity of this "poor prisoner."

But why should Heracles send these women ahead? Certainly not to please Deianira. No, she knows now in her heart why the herald, with whom she has been acquainted for a long time, has waited so long before coming to her. And he is soon to confirm her fears when he admits that it was to spare her too much pain that he has remained silent. The princess Iole has been sent on ahead to leave Deianira in no doubt as to who is to be the new mistress of his household.

We learn that, out of love for Iole, Heracles has defeated a whole kingdom. And now that he has survived this feat, he is going to settle down to enjoy a new *dolce vita*. After all, why should he share his life with a woman past her prime? Deianira cunningly draws all this information from the herald; she tells him he need not spare her feelings, for she knows life, she knows men. She even feigns pity for the girl, in whom she sees a reflection of her own youth. The girl will not fare otherwise than Deianira herself, for such is the fate of woman. Heracles is nothing if not the typical man, going from one woman to the next; he is the philanderer *par excellence*.

Deianira speaks almost slightingly of him, and says that he will soon tire of this new love and return to her. After all, this is not the first time that this has happened. But in her heart she knows differently, for Heracles had never before brought his women home. Moreover, the oracle had said that Heracles would never again leave home. Iole says nothing. (In fact, her role is a silent one throughout the whole play). As the herald conducts Heracles' new beloved and the other women into the palace, Deianira confides in the Chorus: "I cannot be angry with him, having gone through it a hundred times. But this he cannot do to me; to live with the girl under one roof, to sleep with her under one sheet."

She will be Heracles' wife in name only. The young girl will be wife in *fact*. For how can she compete with a girl in the bloom of youth?

As Deianira reflects on her sorry plight, she remembers a love potion given to her a long time ago. Heracles had once entrusted her to the care of the centaur Nessus, instructing him to carry her across a river. While doing so the centaur had been unduly familiar with Deianira's person, whereupon Heracles had let fly with one of his poisoned arrows, striking him in the heart. Nessus' dying words to Deianira had described how she could prepare a potion capable of winning the love of any man if she took his blood, dried it, and then rubbed it into the garment of the man in question.

Deianira's total despair sways her otherwise clear-headed self to resort to these means. "Is it foolish?" she asks the girls. She can but try; after all, she has no other choice. So she anoints a robe with the love philter and, putting it into a casket, entrusts it to the herald, bidding him give it to Heracles as a coming-home present. She then withdraws, leaving the Chorus alone on stage.

After a rather joyful choral song, a distraught Deianira rushes from the house. There has been a terrible sign: the piece of wool with which she had daubed the philter on Heracles' garment, has shriveled up and totally disappeared. Meanwhile the blood itself is bubbling evilly. Suddenly it dawns on her that the "love potion" is really a poison. What else would Nessus, dying from Heracles' arrow, have had in mind other than to take his revenge somehow? She is now potentially a murderer and she vows to give up her own life should Heracles perish because of her.

Scarcely has she finished speaking than Hyllus enters with the inevitable news. His report is full of pathos and he, too, is again very much moved by the events he has witnessed and is now describing. Heracles' sufferings are graphically detailed, and we learn that even though he suffered terrible torments and agonies his great strength remained undiminished. He had snatched up the unfortunate herald, who had unwittingly brought disaster, and hurled him against a rock. The assembled populace groaned fearfully as the hero raved. Hyllus now points to his mother: she is the one who murdered him. May the Furies punish her! It was all her plan.

Without a word, Deianira runs into the house. Soon after, the Nurse enters and tells how her mistress has just committed suicide by throwing herself upon Heracles' sword.

Heracles

We are now ready for the events of the last part of the tragedy. A choral song once again provides the transition and describes how the oracle has come true. The blame is laid at the feet of Aphrodite. Heracles' sufferings have, indeed, now come to an end. One might have expected a raging, roaring hero racked by pain. But when a long procession slowly enters, the body on the litter is tranquil. Heracles is completely covered; only his bearded face is visible. Hyllus comes from the house, and, seeing the apparently lifeless body, vents his grief in loud moans. An old man bids him keep quiet since Heracles is sleeping, but his warning is too late.

Heracles awakes and is immediately so tortured by the poison that he cries out in rage and pain. Will no one end his sufferings? He exhorts Hyllus to plunge his sword into his putrid body, and he curses Deianira. Sinking back exhausted, he calls upon Hades to send him quick death. The Chorus draws back with a shudder, and an antiphony now follows.

With a tremendous effort the hero suppresses his agony in order to make clear both to himself and to all the full extent of what has befallen him. Must he be so sorely afflicted after all that he has achieved on earth? Here he lies, sobbing like a girl, ruined by a woman. He asks his son to bring Deianira before him so that he may take revenge on her.

Hyllus hesitates and Heracles throws off the covers so that all may see his putrefying body. The sunlight only intensifies his pain, however, and once more he gives expression to his sufferings: "O my hands, my hands, how many have you conquered? And now paralyzed, you are torn to shreds, ruined by blind Áte. Get her, so that she learn and let all others know that I punished the evil, and that I punish them in death." Again he asks for the "one who did this to me." He will show the world that even dying he punishes evil.

Hyllus now reports his mother's suicide—which is clear proof that she is not responsible for Heracles' lingering death. At the mention of Nessus, Heracles suddenly remembers another old oracle (the oracles are of Sophocles' invention) which forecast that he would be killed by someone already dead. Everything now fits together. The end to his sufferings is simply death.

Heracles now expresses his last wish. It underlines the character Sophocles gave his hero—a mixture of greatness and brutality. He bids Hyllus take him to the top of Mount Oeta and there erect a funeral pyre. Hyllus is to lay his father's *living* body on this pyre and put to it the flaming brand of a pine torch. "Let there be no tears, no mourning," Heracles commands. But Hyllus is horrified at this request. Does his father realize that he is asking him to be his murderer?

This is to be Heracles' last deed, so to speak. His death is to be a sign to both gods and men; the flames are to rise up to Zeus himself. The gods may have destroyed that part of him which is mortal, but they have not touched that which has made him the first man of the world, namely his indomitable will to action.

Heracles then relentlessly extracts from his son a promise to marry the girl who had been the indirect cause of his mother's death. Even on the verge of death Heracles is possessed of an irresistible power over men.

But his last words are not the last of the tragedy. These fall to Hyllus: Monstrous is the gods' unmindfulness. They sire sons, and while they are praised as fathers, they look unmoved at our sufferings. What shall happen cannot be foreseen. What happens now is our woe—and the gods' shame.

Never in Greek tragedy has there been such a grave

indictment of the superpower exercised over man by the pitiless gods. Even the greatest of men cannot escape destruction when the gods ordain it. The play is an exhortation to all, both the fortunate and the unfortunate, to reflect that here the son of a god has slain a mortal only to have the gods bring about his own downfall by means of this selfsame mortal. The action to this play is hence brought to a full circle; only one aspect shines out beyond: the defiance of a hero at the point of death.

The play is constructed to lead with steadily heightening tension up to the final climax. Though he first appears late in the play, the presence of Heracles is felt throughout. What would Deianira be without him? But how much of a man is he without Deianira? Her inner excitment rises steadily throughout as each step she takes brings her closer to him, and even her last act is his doing. The life of a woman founders because of the life style of the hero; the greater the hero, the unhappier the woman who loves him and who has to share his life. Deianira becomes Heracles' murderer but remains innocent of the deed. Heracles, on the other hand, does, in a sense, kill Deianira.

W. W. Schlegel, the Romantic critic and German translator of Shakespeare, was repelled by the grim conclusion. But our own age—like Shakespeare's—has witnessed so many atrocities, that these horrors are readily understandable. Clearly convinced of the play's contemporary relevance, Ezra Pound underlined this fact by translating *The Women of Trachis* into a present-day vernacular often verging on slang.

It would be wrong to criticize his use of the vernacular, for Sophocles' dialogue also makes use of everyday speech. Pound uses the vernacular to great effect by placing such passages in direct contrast to the choral songs, which are highly poetic in tone. He saw in the drama analogies to the Japanese *Noh* plays, and he interpreted the tragedy as tracing the transformation of the hero from man into god, calling it a "god-dance." There is, however, no trace of this in Sophocles' play, and Pound has sometimes been taken to task for not even attempting to show Heracles as worthy of elevation to divine status. The criticism is unjust, for with typical astuteness, Pound purposely avoided the one point that resists contemporary relevance.

Sophocles was perfectly justified in presupposing in his audience a belief in the reality of this superman as a distinct possibility of mortal existence. However, posterity has not only glorified this man of action—simultaneously a purger of evil and a man of brutal violence—it has deified him. In Sophocles' view it is imperative that Heracles die as a mortal. The dramatist reminds posterity that the gods conceived of a most cruel death for this superman deified by mortals. Heracles' last deed is only great if it opposes the gods with a distinctly human action, the action of a man who takes his fame with him to his death. The play does not prove this fame; it assumes it. It depicts the hero as wicked and suffering; it gives him at the moment of death a greatness which is worthy of a life that no longer seems real to us.

Oedipus the King

The background to this play is twofold: there are those events which are known to the characters on the stage and others known only to the audience. The former events are rapidly described in the opening scenes. The revelation of the latter is the concern of the action of the play. Sophocles directed attention not so much at the events themselves as at the significance they have for the characters, and at an interpretation of the characters' behavior. The modern director is therefore well advised somehow to communicate to the audience the background events not described in the opening scenes.

There are in addition some historical events of which the modern audience should be aware. A few years before the play was first performed Athens had been hit by plague, just as Thebes is in the play itself. After some thirteen years as head of state, the great statesman Pericles, a contemporary of Sophocles, had been ousted from power. When the situation became

An overall view of the amphitheater at Epidaurus during
a festival of classical Greek drama.
GREEK NATIONAL TOURIST OFFICE

Opposite, Alexis Minotis in the title role of *Oedipus the King*. Above we see him in an Epidaurus production of *Oedipus at Colonus*. Minotis and his wife, the late Katina Paxinou, were responsible for many remarkable productions from the classical repertory.

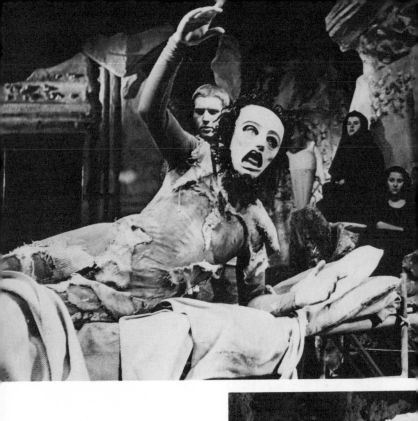

Edmund Saussen as Heracles in a 1959 staging of *The Women of Trachis* at the Landstheater, Darmstadt, Germany. The production was based on Ezra Pound's adaptation.
PIT LUDWIG

Below, Irene Papas in Michael Cacoyannis' production of *Antigone*. "You plunged from the highest peak of daring and now you face the law."
GREEK NATIONAL TOURIST OFFICE

Lee Grant plays the title role in *Electra* in the New York Shakespeare Festival production in 1964. It was the first non-Shakespeare play offered by the group.
ZODIAC

desperate he was re-elected, only to be almost immediately snatched away by the plague. Sophocles did not tamper with the myth in any way, but he did add several details that were designed to give the familiar figures an immediacy for his audience. Anyone concerned with making the play more vital for modern audiences is faced with a similar task.

Background I

The plague is raging in Thebes, and Oedipus, king of Thebes, is deeply concerned. Fifteen years earlier the city had lived in terror of the Sphinx, but Oedipus, coming from Delphi, had solved the monster's riddle and thereby rid Thebes of this horrible curse. In deep gratitude the city had offered Oedipus the hand of the recently widowed Queen Jocasta and with it, of course, the throne. For these many years he had ruled Thebes wisely and well. His marriage had been blessed with four children—two boys and two girls—and then the plague had come.

The people are in despair. Creon, the queen's brother and one of the most powerful men in the city, has been sent to Delphi to consult the oracle. In such a situation mere mortals are powerless and only the gods can help. During the night before the action of the play begins, the skies were lit by the flames from the funeral pyres of plague victims. The priests have called upon the people to support Creon's mission with communal prayer at the altars. The cries of lament and the imploring voices of the suppliants penetrate to the very palace.

Background II

Jocasta, Oedipus' wife, is in reality his mother. Her first husband, Laius, son of Labdacus and great-grandson of the founder of the city, Cadmus, had been killed whilst traveling through the mountains at about the same time that Oedipus had vanquished the Sphinx. In point of fact, he had been killed by his own son Oedipus.

It had happened like this. An oracle had once prophesied to the young couple that the son Jocasta was about to bear would kill his father and sleep with his mother. Understandably horrified at this news, Laius had therefore arranged for the child to be exposed on a mountainside, where it would presumably perish. However, a herdsman had taken the infant to a childless royal couple who ruled in Corinth, on the other side of the mountains. Only a few people knew that Oedipus, who grew up as a crown prince, loved and admired by everyone, was not the true son of King Polybus and Queen Merope.

When Oedipus was about twenty he heard unsettling rumors about himself, and therefore decided to visit the Delphic oracle. But the oracle proved to be anything but reassuring: he would kill his father and lie with his mother. Horrified, he decided against returning to Corinth, where, as far as he was concerned, his parents were awaiting him.

On the road from Delphi which took him through the mountains near Thebes, he came across a chariot containing an elderly man (Laius) and his arms bearers. The former haughtily ordered Oedipus to make way for him. Oedipus refused and a contest ensued in which the young hero killed the old man and all but one of his companions. He then continued on his way until he met the Sphinx.

At this point the events outlined in Background I begin. Just as Oedipus was totally ignorant of the fact that the man in the chariot had been Laius, his father, so, too, were the Thebans ignorant of the fact that the son of Laius and Jocasta was still alive. Only gradually do the characters penetrate to the facts behind this veil of ignorance. The audience, however, is from the very beginning aware of the true facts and even of the events to come. Since Oedipus' fate is known, a tragic irony pervades the action and the speeches.

The Plague and the Oracle

It is dawn in front of the royal palace. The groans and hymns of the suppliants can be heard behind the scene. A procession enters from the left to the sound of muffled drums and mournful music. Venerable priests in long robes accompany children and youths carrying olive branches and wreaths, the emblems of suppliants (*Hikesía*, the right to beg protection, is a hallowed right sanctified by both church and state; the persecuted may resort to it; in this case those persecuted by the plague call upon the gods for protection.)

The procession gradually nears the altars before the palace and moves pointedly toward that of Apollo behind the columns of the right wing which projects into the orchestra. The children and the youths decorate the altars with their wreaths, and then, as the music dies away they sink onto the steps in postures of supplication with one arm raised towards the altar and the other holding the olive branch. The central doors of the palace are thrown open and Oedipus appears holding his scepter and followed by his guard.

He wears a beardless mask and the long, white robes of the ruling monarch. His manner indicates impulsiveness, imperiousness, and excitement. On seeing the suppliants cowering before the altar, he realizes what has brought them here; but since nobody apparently takes the slightest notice of him, he asks for an explanation. "O my children, youngest generation of the ancient line of Cadmus, why are you sitting here at the altar before me, bearing olive branches wreathed with wool? The city is filled with the scent of incense, filled with the sounds of hymns and mourning. I do not think it right, my children, that I should learn of this from others."

At this point the audience learns that the reason for such lamentations is the plague. The priest adds that the gods alone can save Thebes, but that since Oedipus is the greatest among men and since he was previously the instrument of the city's salavation when he had delivered Thebans from the Sphinx, might he not be the one to save them on this occasion, too? He ends his speech on a desperate and almost accusing note: "O greatest of mortals, lift up our state again, rescue us again."

As the speech rises to its climax, the suppliants gradually join in his request with their cries and gestures.

Oedipus makes no attempt to conceal how deeply he has been hurt by the priest's words, for he has heard clearly enough the reproach behind them: why had he not already come to their aid? His reply demonstrates his greatness, coming, as it does, from the man who lives for his people and whose grief at this catastrophe far and away eclipses theirs, since each of them suffers his own pain, but he suffers for them all. But there is a limit to his powers. The mind that was able to solve the Sphinx's riddle cannot discover the reason for the plague inflicted on Thebes.

Oedipus grieves, then, not only for his people but also because of his inability to devise a solution for their salvation. The extent to which the reputation of this man—whom, by his own admission, the world calls "the Great"—is based on his intellectual capacities is soon made clear. It now becomes obvious, moreover, that he has to acknowledge the pestilence as an inexplicable blow from without, from an inconceivable fate to which all earthly beings are exposed.

Poring over the problem and a possible solution, Oedipus had painfully come to the conclusion that there was but one last hope and he had acted accordingly. Surely Creon must, by now, have returned from Delphi with an answer from that god who alone could save them, from the god who had inflicted the plague upon the city. As he impatiently asks where Creon has been all this time, a small group of travelers comes on the scene. In great excitement the crowd surges forward, buoyed up with hope, for they have seen that Creon is crowned with a laurel wreath, signifying good news.

The excited people fall back, making way for the two men, as Oedipus hurries down the steps saying: "Prince, my kinsman, son of Menoeceus, what word have you brought us from the god?" Creon's answer at once reveals the difference in character between these two men. He enigmatically suggests that there is good news, but wonders whether they should not retire within rather than speak before the assembled crowd. Oedipus indignantly rebukes him. Since his grief is based on the people's sorry plight and since the news concerns them first and foremost, Creon should speak here before them. Step by step Oedipus now begins to block all means of escape from the trap into which, as we know, he has fallen. Creon reveals the typically obscure Delphic oracle: Drive out the land's pollution. Do not continue nourishing an incurable ulcer.

What follows is interpretation, showing that Creon had probably discussed the matter with the priests in Delphi. The "pollution" is clearly the pestilence, which was sent as a punishment for the unexpiated murder, indeed regicide, of Laius. Oedipus wonders why the murder had not already been punished by his people. As he sets himself up as a kind of special investigator into this crime, the audience, knowing the truth, cannot repress a shudder. All citizens of the city are under suspicion—all except Oedipus, that is, for he did not arrive in the polis until after the death of Laius, whom, so far as he knew, he had never even met.

Apparently unassailable in his integrity, he begins his investigations and asks Creon what is known of the murderers (the attentive will immediately note his use of the plural)? Where can they be? Creon concludes, logically enough, that they must be in Thebes, for that is where the plague is. After further questions Oedipus ascertains that there is one alive, who was present at the slaying and that there was no investigation. It must then have been a political murder and Laius must have been murdered at the instigation of his political enemies. These same plotters must have insured that no investigation should uncover the assassins. Creon disagrees. It is the Sphinx who is to be blamed. That creature of riddles led the Thebans to set aside all thoughts of the dark past and to devote themselves to what lay at hand.

At the mention of the Sphinx, Oedipus breaks in to say that he will now solve this riddle, too, and be the salavation of the city. He calls a meeting of the assembly, and as the suppliants rise and leave, Creon follows Oedipus into the palace.

The Edict and the Seer

The Chorus enters from the left, or from the city. It is the council of old men representing the people's assembly. As befits people of an older generation they hold conservative views; they are both venerable and old-fashioned. They bring with them onto the stage further lamentation, and they give vent to their feelings with song and dance. Added to their fear of the pestilence is yet another fear: apprehension at the consequences of the oracle. Just as their outpourings reach a climax, Oedipus and his followers enter from the palace.

Without a word he watches the old men, who seem almost possessed, and listens to their impassioned words. After a while they recover their senses and take up positions more appropriate of a council before its king. Oedipus fittingly reprimands them for their witless frenzy. "You say prayers, but would do better to listen to my words." He makes a proclamation containing four main counts: (1) Everything pertaining to the murder must be reported to me. (2) Those who implicate themselves shall be guaranteed safe conduct from the polis. (3) Anyone revealing the identity of the murderer will be rewarded. (4) Anyone found guilty of concealing information about the murder shall be banished from the polis. (Ironically, Oedipus now repeatedly speaks of the murderer in the singular!)

So much as to Oedipus' official duty. He now makes it clear just how much he is personally committed to solving this crime. In substantiating all that is contained in the edict he heaps curse upon curse until he reaches the ominous climax:

> May the murderer, whether he lies hidden in solitary guilt or had partners in his crime, may he pass the rest of his wretched life surrounded by evil equal to his wrong-doing. And I vow that, if he should come to share my hearth unknown to me, I shall pray I suffer the same curse I have just now called down upon all others.

Turning to the Chorus he further asserts:

> And since now I hold the royal power that once he held, and have his bed and wife as well—and since, if he had not been unfortunate in his hope for children we would have been kin through common offspring of the same wife, but, as it happened, an evil fell upon his head—I shall, therefore, take it upon myself to avenge his death as though he were my own father.

And, as if to make this terrible curse still more terrible, he lists all the kings of Thebes right back to the very beginning, Laius and all his ancestors, the line which stretches down to the present and whose last name must, by rights, be his own. Finally, he calls down the plague, or a fate even worse, on those who do not support him, the city and Díke the goddess of justice in his bid to save the city.

A short dialogue between Oedipus and the Chorus prepares the audience for the entry of Tiresias, whom Oedipus, on the advice of Creon, has already summoned. The sight of the hoary, blind seer feeling his way with his crooked staff and leaning on a boy for support never fails to have the desired and customary effect on the audience. Tiresias, wearing the white-haired and white-bearded mask of the old man and the gold-embroidered priest's garb, is greeted with deep reverence. Even Oedipus turns immediately to him with great respect and, following the example of the old men of the council, he kneels down in supplication: "We are in your hands."

This scene is magnificently constructed. Sophocles has Tiresias hesitate, even turn as if to go. Of course, he knows the whole truth and will finally come out with it. Why else has he come? For the moment, however, the blind man's vision is enough to seal his lips. The scene demonstrates just how much tension there is between the man of god and the man of reason, a tension which is scarcely concealed. But Tiresias could hardly have anticipated what now happens: this man of reason kneels down and delivers himself into his hands. In the name of the polis he submits to the holy powers which the seer represents. Had Oedipus stood up to him as an opponent, Tiresias would have told him everything he knew without any scruples. As it is, he now finds himself unable to expose this humble man to his fate. "Allow me to go home, for you will bear your burden more easily, and I mine, if you let me go," is all he says.

Strangely enough, it is precisely this forebearance on Tiresias' part that now forces Oedipus into the role of opponent. Still kneeling, he cries: "You do not speak with fairness or with loyalty to this city that nurtured you if you withhold your word of prophecy."

The old man stands and looks fixedly back at the suppliants: "I will not speak out the evils that I know nor reveal that these evils are yours as well." When told that if he knows and will not speak he is in effect bringing destruction on the polis, the seer replies: "I will not bring grief upon myself or upon you. Why do you persist in asking me for what you will never learn from me?"

Oedipus now openly tries to provoke Tiresias into revealing what he knows and even goes so far as to accuse the old man of having had his part in the crime and of now remaining silent to conceal the deed. This is too much for Tiresias who, much to the Chorus' consternation and horror, finally comes out with: "I charge you then to stand by the accusation with your own tongue. You are the one; you are the guilty wretch who brought pollution to this land."

Sophocles has delineated the character of his hero in such a way that he is always able to retire to within himself at moments of great emotional intensity and reflect upon events until he regains clarity. This part of the play is no exception. Oedipus is convinced of his innocence. But he knows, on the other hand, what it would mean should Tiresias prove to be correct. He must accordingly become master of the political situation, and he goes about it in a cool and rational manner.

His argument is that Tiresias is not speaking as a prophet. He is part of a plot headed by Creon, and just as Laius had been murdered, so now is Oedipus to be removed. Obviously, these people wish to seize power. But the verbal struggle with the seer rises to a breaking point. Every sentence Oedipus utters is answered by some further awful revelation:

> I say you are the murderer of the king for whose murderer you are searching. . . . I say that you are living in shameful sin with the one closest to you and you do not see the evil. . . . Your fate is not to fall by my hand. It is Apollo who will pronounce judgment on you.

And yet Oedipus is still in possession of a convincing argument: where was this man with his holy powers when the Sphinx was terrorizing the land? Did *he*, perhaps, solve the riddle?

> But I came, Oedipus, all untrained, and brought her to an end. I arrived at the right answer by my wits, not by the birds' portents. And yet I am the one you are attempting to overthrow thinking you will take your place beside the throne of Creon.

This is why this whole action against him has started, this is why he is being branded as unclean. The oracle, as well as the pestilence, has come at a most opportune moment, fitting very well into the general scheme.

In order to have Oedipus leave the scene as victor in his people's eyes, the poet has the Chorus sing at the end of the scene: "Never will he be found guilty." But meanwhile the scene is not yet at an end for Oedipus. Tiresias has a weapon of tremendous power, and only one person on the stage joins the audience in knowing how unerringly deeply strikes the question: "Do you know at all who you are? You have eyes but see not the evil that surrounds you, nor where you are living, nor who shares the house with you. Do you in fact know your lineage?"

It is not until several verses later that Oedipus reveals just how hurt he is by this thrust. As the old man is about to leave, he once again mentions Oedipus' "parents." The king is visibly shaken: "Say, what do you know of my parents?" And as he says it, something which has been lying dormant all these years breaks out again with all its nagging pain: the uncertainty of his birth.

The old man's answer is obscure as far as all those on the stage are concerned but perfectly clear to the audience: "This day will show your birth as well as death." The seer's exit is as hesitant as his entrance had been; he begins to go, then turns again and finally flings these last words in Oedipus' face:

> That man—the one you have been seeking all this time, threatening and denouncing him as the murderer of Laius—that man is right here. He was called a stranger who settled in our city. But soon he will be shown to be a native of Thebes, born in this city, yet he will not rejoice at this good fortune. No, blind and no longer endowed with sight, a beggar and no longer rich, he will set off for a strange land, feeling his way with his staff. And he will be disclosed to be both brother and father of the children who share his house, both son and husband of the woman who gave birth, and successor to his father and his murderer as well.

And with these words the terrible truth is fully revealed, and yet it is so terrible that it seems incredible.

After Tiresias' exit, Oedipus goes back into the palace. The Chorus carries on the mood of ominous disaster: "Dreadful things the seer has stirred up." But then, even a seer is only human, after all; only the gods are omniscient. And before any clear and definite proof is given we side with Oedipus.

Creon the Traitor, and the Queen

Rumors have driven Creon out of the palace into the city streets. He is without followers and without weapons. He asks the old men to tell him what Oedipus has accused him of. They are unwilling to commit themselves to any great extent and simply say that Oedipus' words were probably spoken in anger. How should they be able to explain the words and actions of princes? At this point Oedipus, followed by his body-guard, storms angrily out of the palace: "Is it you? Can it be that you have come back? Can you have the daring and the face to come near this house of mine— you the recognized murderer of its master?"

Creon protests his innocence and demands a hearing. In a tremendous battle of words they fight it out, blow for blow, line by line. So convinced is Oedipus that he is the victim of Creon's treason that he badgers Creon as if he were a prosecuting attorney exposing the weaknesses of a guilty defendant. Had Creon not advised him to send for Tiresias? Was no investigation made when Laius was killed? Was Tiresias around then? Why had he not offered then the information he offers now?

But it is Creon who wins the approval of the Chorus. In his eloquent rebuttal he reaffirms his innocence. Now, as coregent, he is equal in power to Jocasta and Oedipus. Why would he want the actual crown in a time of trouble?

This exchange is more than a mere battle of words; it is a trial. Oedipus' throne, indeed his very existence, hangs in the balance. He must therefore be able to refute the accusations made against him. On the other hand, Creon knows the penalty for high treason: death. He realizes that Oedipus cannot now retract his accusations, so his only chance lies in getting the council of elders on his side. If Oedipus were to act against the wishes of the polis, it would be tantamount to tyranny, and whatever shortcomings Oedipus' rule might show in certain individual cases, it is, nonetheless, absolutely opposed to tyranny.

Creon, therefore, makes no effort to refute the charges laid against him; neither does he attempt to make a declaration of solidarity with Oedipus and against Tiresias. Instead, he argues more generally and more persuasively. Why should he, Creon, who enjoys respect, wealth, and, moreover, as coregent, possesses power, attempt to take upon his own shoulders the burden and cares of the king? Playing the role of the simple, honest man, Creon is successful. He even goes so far as to tell Oedipus that if any proof can be found of his plotting with Tiresias to kill the king, he will willingly accept the death penalty, indeed, he will even ask for it.

The Chorus gives its backing to these arguments, and Creon sees that he has won. Oedipus stands isolated. Once again the battle of words rises to a climax. When he still calls for Creon's death, Creon questions his reason, his sanity:

> CREON: But if you have no sense at all?
> OEDIPUS: Still I must rule.
> CREON: Not if you are ruling badly.

In despair almost, Oedipus cries out "O, city, city!" The pathos of these words can only be appreciated if we remember that they come from the man who was once the city's salvation, and who has, ever since, given his all for the good of the polis.

The sounds of this intense argument have caused the queen to come apprehensively rushing out of the palace. Jocasta, accompanied by her servants and dressed in royal robes with a diadem over her mask, enters from the left and throws herself between her husband and brother:

> For shame! Why are you waging this ill-advised battle of words? Are you not ashamed to air your private feelings when our land is sick with the plague?

She has all the authority of an older, maturer person (as Oedipus' mother she is in all likelihood at least twenty years his senior) and her presence is magnificently regal. With an urgency stemming from her anxiety for the lives of her brother and husband opposing each other in a life-and-death struggle, she issues her orders:"Go inside now—and you, Creon, go home—and stop making so much over a little argument!"

Emotions run high, there is music and antiphony. The Chorus tries to intercede and suddenly everyone is earnestly beseeching the hero not to add to their troubles yet another disaster in the form of general anarchy (for it is quite clear that Creon and his followers will not give up without a struggle). As they kneel down, desperate, in supplication, the music comes to an end and all is silent.

When Oedipus begins to speak again, it is clear that

something within him has snapped. But when once again Creon flares up, Oedipus imperiously dismisses him.

After Creon leaves, Oedipus remains with Jocasta, who wants to know what has happened, and the Chorus, which exhorts the royal couple "to leave it where it ended." But how could Oedipus do that? With deepest pathos he expresses his resentment at the Chorus for having swayed his judgment and calmed his wrath. Creon—the embodiment of evil—is against him, but so are the well-meaning good people. The polis has deserted him.

In the depths of his soul a decision of the greatest significance has been made. Had he ignored the will of the people and sentenced Creon to death, he would have found himself compelled to rule as a tyrant. This would have gone against both his will and his better judgment. Now that he has been forced to give way, his mind turns once more to the supranatural forces that envelop and limit man's insight and power. No matter how inconceivable the accusation made against him may seem, it is, nonetheless, within the realm of *possibility*, just as the plague is, just as the desertion of the polis is. He has lost all confidence in himself and in his own powers. And he is never again to regain it, unless perhaps with his last, ghastly action. The song with which the Chorus leaves the stage sounds like bitter irony: "You were the savior of our land, remain its good helmsman!"

Man and Wife, Mother and Son

The following scene marks the center and the climax of the tragic action. The uncovering of all the events of the past, which now rapidly takes place, is somewhat ironic in that it occurs against the will and without the knowledge of those who are speaking. When Jocasta hears what the seer has said, she is jubilant because she is certain in her own mind that this cannot be true. That son who has supposedly killed his father was taken from her as a tiny baby and left to perish. How could Laius have possibly been killed, there where the three roads meet, by someone who no longer exists?

But when Oedipus hears her mention where Laius had been killed, he gives a start, for it was at precisely such a place that he had killed the arrogant stranger and his followers. As events take this uncanny turn, Oedipus begins to tremble: "O dear Jocasta, as I listened to your words, uneasiness seized my spirit, turbulence struck my heart."

All this is beyond Jocasta's comprehension, yet, as a woman and a mother she is able to perceive that something awful is going on in Oedipus' mind. She exerts all her powers to distract him, but to little avail. Oedipus, in his gradual realization of the truth, begins to see how cruelly the gods have treated him:

> O Zeus, what has your will done to me? O wretch that I am! It seems that I have just called down a terrible curse upon my own head and knew not that I did so. And I have dread fears that the old seer is not truly blind.

Finally, he gives her an account of all the events leading up to his arrival in Thebes from Delphi—why he had left Corinth, and what had happened at the place where those three roads met. And even as he gives this account his unconscious realization of the awful truth is completed; he is now fully aware of his true identity.

> If there was any tie of kinship between this man and Laius, what man is then more wretched than I? What mortal then more hateful to the Gods?

Oedipus now knows all: the murder alone could not move him to such words. After all, he had killed in self-defense. But what if he has killed his own father and has gone on to commit incest? What remains to him now? In recognizing just what he has done, and in coming to a full awareness of his action, Oedipus realizes that the facts must be revealed to the people, for such is his honest and noble character. Only by doing this will he be able to atone for his deeds.

Jocasta has not progressed this far in her reasoning but is still grasping desperately at one last remaining straw. One of Laius' companions had managed to escape and, on his return, reported that there had been several assassins. This man is still alive and could testify. But the audience can have no doubt as to how he would testify, for Jocasta has already unwittingly revealed how things stand. When this man had returned to Thebes and seen Oedipus on the throne at Jocasta's side, he had begged to be allowed to retire to the mountains as a herdsman.

Nevertheless, Oedipus agrees that this man should be sent for so that he might be absolutely positive of all the facts. But a yawning abyss is opening up between the royal couple. If Oedipus is Laius' son, then he is guilty of both patricide and incest. As for Jocasta, she is guilty of incest and attempted infanticide. Bowed down with sorrow, deserted by all, and filled with dread, Oedipus allows himself to be led up the palace steps by Jocasta. His steps are labored. She walks with him, taking his arm in her hand. As they enter the palace, the door closes behind them with a crash.

The Witnesses

The old men's choral song rises in intensity. The power of destiny rules over us all. It strikes tyrants who have no respect for law, it punishes those guilty of hubris and those whose fingers itch for untouchable things:

> That man can ever hope to shield himself against the avenging arrows of the gods . . . ? No more shall I travel to the sacred temple at earth's center, to Abae's shrine, or to Olympia if the true word of the gods is not made manifest to all men in their trouble. O king, if you are rightly called king, O Zeus, king over all, may it not go unnoticed by you and your everlasting might. For the oracles surrounding Laius, spoken long ago, fade into forgetfulness and now are laid aside. Nowhere is Apollo made bright with honors, for the worship of the gods is faltering.

There is ambiguity here, too, and irony is straightaway added to the truth. As if to give the lie to the old men, at this point the door to the women's quarters open and Jocasta appears at the head of a procession bearing olive branches, garlands, and censers. She is on her way to the temple of Apollo (over in the right wing), to offer up those sacrifices which, according to the Chorus, people have forgotten.

True, it is not a ritual sacrifice. Her anxiety for Oedipus, who sits inside the palace brooding moodily and neither speaking nor listening to others, has driven Jocasta to offer up prayers to that god who might best be able to help. As she and her women kneel in supplication at the altar, as prayers are murmured and sacrifices offered, someone enters from the right, or in others words, from foreign parts. It is the first witness. In two short steps the analytical part of the play is brought to an end. In place of the unwilling witness Jocasta, come two witnesses from the outside world. One of them is a complete surprise, the other has been sent for.

A man from Corinth brings news which is both sad and joyful. Oedipus' "father" Polybus has died and the people wish his "son" to take over the throne. Jocasta is delighted: "Be quick and run to the king with the news!" The fact that everything can still, as far as those on the stage are concerned, turn out for the best—for, after all, if Polybus has died a natural death, then how can Oedipus be guilty of patricide—is underlined by the almost comic effect of the messenger. He is an old man of the common folk, a bit of a gossip and somewhat too clever.

Into this deceptively cheerful atmosphere comes Oedipus, who receives the news almost absentmindedly. He is still tortured by the possibility of incest. Jocasta tries to reassure him by saying that many men in their dreams have been wed to their mothers. (It was this passage which inspired Freud to coin the phrase "Oedipus complex.") And now the Corinthian messenger, in an attempt to reassure Oedipus, joyfully and quite unwittingly corroborates all his worst fears. The messenger himself had brought Oedipus as an infant to the court of Corinth after having received him from one of Laius' herdsmen in the hills. They had named him Oedipus because of his pierced ankles —*Oedi-pus* meaning swollen foot.

Apart from Oedipus only one other person on the stage knows what this means: and this is Jocasta. Oedipus pointedly asks her if she knows of this herdsman. Faced with this question, the actor playing the queen has the tremendously difficult task of putting a variety of conflicting emotions into her reaction: there is her general horror at her attempted infanticide, the knowledge that she is her husband's mother; and the awareness that children have been born of their union. To this horror is added apprehension of what Oedipus might now do, and the tension of knowing that there is still hope as long as the others do not know the significance of what has been said and as long as she does not betray anything by her behavior now. As long as the others know nothing, Oedipus can go to Corinth, where no one will be concerned about the whole business. Accordingly, she quickly bids him to pursue the matter no further.

Of course, he would not be Oedipus if he were able to remain silent. He is fully conscious that truth must out and that he must get right to the bottom of the whole affair. How could he live, knowing that certain facts were being concealed? Finally, Jocasta wails her distress:

> JOCASTA: For the sake of the gods, if you value your own life at all, end your search. My misery is enough.
> OEDIPUS: No, I cannot be dissuaded from learning the whole truth.

> JOCASTA: Oh, ill-omened man, may you never
> learn who you are!

Oedipus, however, is adamant and bids them fetch
the herdsman. Shrieking with anguish, Jocasta rushes
into the palace. With grim irony Oedipus calms the
terrified Chorus, who ask: "Why, Oedipus, did the
queen hurry away in such wild distress? I am afraid
now that from this silence there will burst forth a
sudden storm." He tells the old men not to worry
about Jocasta. Clearly her pride is such that she cannot
bear to learn that her husband is not her social equal.

Even as he falls, and he alone knows the extent of
his fall (apart from Jocasta, who is about to commit
suicide), he continues to conduct himself with dignity. The Chorus is so impressed by Oedipus' announcement that he is "a child of Fortune," that it
dances in veritable glee (how cruel Sophocles can be,
when he wishes!). It searches for the gossip behind his
family tree. What nymph was his mother? And what
god his father? Pan, Apollo, Hermes, or Dionysus?

Oedipus listens in silence. His one desire is to bring
his own trial to an end, to arrive at a sentence and
carry it out. But why does he not go into the palace
and take his life, now that he is inwardly certain of all
the facts? Because he is destined to make the facts
public, to see them brought before the polis—the be-
all and end-all of his life—and offered to the world,
which had bestowed upon him fame and power. And
so he stands staring in the direction from which the
herdsman must appear.

When the herdsman arrives, we find that he, too, is
a man of the common folk, but unlike the brash messenger from Corinth, this man is frightened and at-

tempts to conceal his fear behind a taciturn and sullen manner. He is immediately recognized by the Corinthian. Since he seems loath to talk, Oedipus commands that his arms be twisted behind his back. The truth has to be forced from this man, who is silent only because he wishes to preserve the king. Yet, has not Oedipus every reason to hate this man? Why did the herdsman not let the child die rather than give him to the Corinthian?

> I pitied the child, master, and I thought he would take him away to the land from which he himself had come. But the child was saved for the height of shame. For if you are the person this man said you are, you were born to misery!

The utter horror and the tremendous shudder this produces in the Chorus is not captured in words; it is portrayed in actions. The old men, recognizing the full truth in all its implications for the first time, shrink back in terror from this man bearing the stain of such terrible crimes. The Corinthian and the herdsman rush off wailing with anguish. Now all the facts are out, and Oedipus, too, breaks down and moans. When he speaks, his words are pregnant with meaning. No translation can do justice to the original Greek.

> This is the end of me. It has all come true, all is true. O light of my world, may I look upon you now for the last time—I, cursed by my birth, cursed by my marriage, cursed by the killing I have done, am revealed for what I am.

If Sophocles' voice comes through anywhere in the play it is here: if only Oedipus had not been born; but what could he do about it? If only he had not married; but how was he to know whose bed he was to share? And if only he had not killed; but he did not know whom he was killing. All this is spoken by the Chorus after the palace door has closed behind Oedipus:

> Oh, alas, you generations of mortals, what a mere nothing do I reckon your lives to be! For who is there, what man is there who achieves for himself any more happiness than a mere phantom, a fleeting vision that quickly fades away.

As the Chorus brings its song to an end, a servant comes rushing in from the left wing of the palace. Never has the report of a messenger contained such horrors as are now poured forth! To the evils inflicted on the unsuspecting couple by outside forces are added self-inflicted evils. Jocasta has hanged herself over the incestuous marriage bed. On finding her body, Oedipus loosened the noose, tore the fastening brooches from her dress, and stabbed out his eyes with them. As the streams of black blood coursed over his cheeks he said: "The sin I did commit or had committed on me shall never by my eyes be seen."

In answer to the Chorus' question about whether Oedipus has found any ease in his pain, the messenger can only say that his master is even now shouting for someone to unbolt the doors to the palace so that the people of Thebes might see him, marked by the gods and marked by himself.

The bolts are slid back and Oedipus uses his last reserves of strength to slowly push open the door. From the darkness of the interior he staggers toward the light and reveals his mutilated features. There is a tremendous cry. Oedipus' mask has bloody sockets where the eyes should be, and dark streams of blood have run down the cheeks. His robes, his hands, and arms are bespattered with his own blood.

The end of the tragedy, however, is not this abomination, but the answer to it.

The End

The last part of the tragedy begins with the antiphony. Horror and pathos pour forth from the music. Then comes Oedipus' great speech. His powerful lament shows that he clearly understands his wretched plight: "Oh, a dread cloud of darkness has come over me. An unspeakable mist wraps me in dense and overwhelming blackness. Ah, woe is me, again I say, woe is me." The light of his eyes may have been extinguished, but his mental faculties shall never be dimmed.

In the lamentations of the Chorus, Oedipus can discern a note of something he never expected: pity and sympathy. Why did he do himself such a terrible injury? Would it not have been better to have died?

The music dies away and Oedipus' answer is spoken rather than sung: he had made his decision from the moment he realized what the facts were. To take one's own life does not suffice to atone for such a sin. Much greater expiation is needed: "I do not know with what eyes I could look upon my father when I come to Hades, or my hapless mother, since my sins against those two are too great for death by hanging."

This is one means of attaining "greater expiation." The other is connected with the polis. What meaning would his earlier life devoted to his people have if he did not now carry out that punishment with which he had threatened the murderer? No, he would have to carry out this threat, and, indeed, increase the punishment two- or even three-fold. If he could destroy his sense of hearing, his wretched body would be completely cut off. And now, spoken in his tragic isolation, comes the key sentence: To live beyond the reach of hurt is sweet.

All has been taken from him—happiness, honor, power—except the power of the intellect, the power of reflection, of knowledge, of passing judgment. The judgment in this case must be applied to himself: "Quickly, for the love of the gods, hide me somewhere far from here, or slay me, or hurl me into the sea that you may never see me again."

He will not take his own life. They, the people, shall do it. They must carry out the will of the gods, a will which is beyond normal powers of comprehension. His final words to them are, for all their wretchedness, still the words of a monarch: "Come, condescend to touch the remnants of a man. Come, don't be afraid— it is I who must bear the burden of sins no other mortal can."

Before the tragedy can come to an end, Oedipus has to be toppled from even this degree of self-confidence. Creon returns from the city. He has clearly taken over power: he bears the attributes of the king and has a bodyguard in attendance. Oedipus stares blindly into the direction from which the sound of marching and weapons comes. Immediately he realizes that all is not yet over, for he is in the hands of the man whom he once accused of murder. He will have to *beg* this man for that which he has just *demanded* of the people. When he enters Creon behaves monstrously. He tells

Oedipus that he has not come to mock or to reproach him for evils past, but he asks the elders to show some respect for the sun, as lord of light, and bids them remove this horrible sight to within. But before this can happen Oedipus implores Creon to do one thing for his own good and the good of his people: "Cast me from this land; send me in all haste to a place where no human voice will ever reach me."

This, Creon says, he would long since have done, had he not been compelled to first ask the god the course of action to be taken: "Now even you will trust the god." Oedipus asks Creon to see that Jocasta is properly buried, again asks that he be banished from the land, and begs Creon to look after his two small daughters.

At this moment Ismene and Antigone are brought (at Creon's instigation) from the palace and led up to their blind father, who embraces them. The pity evoked by this touching group comes pouring forth from all those gathered round. Request and prophecy alike give way to song, after Oedipus calls his children to these "brother's hands." And, indeed, as long as the relationship is one of brother to sisters, the little children are not damned. He entrusts them to Creon as if it has already been arranged that he should now leave, or better still, *may* leave, and asks him to look after them: "Touch my hand, noble Creon, and say yes."

Creon gives no answer, neither does he take the hand. Slowly Oedipus lets his outstretched hand drop. May the children's life prove happier than their father's. But Creon has had enough and interrupts. Oedipus has shed enough tears. Now he is to seclude himself in the palace. Such is Creon's decision, a decision which Oedipus must accept. Once again he pulls himself together and begs to be sent into exile, but Creon again says that such a decision can only be made by the god. Unsatisfied, Oedipus repeats his request, and Creon rebukes him: "Do not try to be master in everything, for even the mastery you did have did not follow you all your life."

Clearly, Oedipus must forthwith learn to obey rather than to issue commands. His future life will be devoid of power. He shall live out the rest of his life without any rights, a beggar, blind. Creon urges him into the palace. The doors are closed and we are left with the words of the departing Chorus ringing in our ears: "Let no mortal be counted happy until death has made him safe from misfortune."

The unmatched greatness of this tragedy lies in its timeless conception. The structure seems to stem from the strict logical sequence of events; but one would be equally justified in saying that the events follow the strict logic of the structure. There is no scene, no character, no part of the action, indeed nothing which could be omitted. Each line is spoken with the one goal in mind, and this goal shines through every line.

The poet interpreted a mythological event for his own age, and just as there was relevance in the myth for that particular age so also is there relevance in his play for us today. The fall of a great man is described. His greatness lies in his moral character and his mind. Sophocles shows how even great intelligence is inadequate when it is pitted against the mystery of the great power surrounding and controlling all human existence.

It is not, however, a tragedy of fate. A heroic and tragic possibility of human existence is realized in the way Oedipus meets defeat: he answers back, he resists,

he endures. Even in moments of most extreme humili-
ation, Oedipus is not deserted by that power through
which he came to the fore: his powers of perception.
He realizes that he is doomed, but his commitment to
the full truth is not impaired by his doom.

The individual case of this hero achieves its full
dimension by virtue of the fact that Oedipus is part of
a stage world which represents the greater world in
general (a mythical, yet relevant world, relevant both
then and now). Though the inconceivable power of
the gods strikes one individual of the polis, Oedipus is
unthinkable without the polis, just as the polis is unthinkable without him. It is precisely from this dimension that the dramatist achieves the dimensions of the
play's structure: the play's structure is also the structure of a world. The possibilities of human existence
are both put in order and played off one against the
other. In view of the necessary concentration, it is
truly miraculous that each person who walks onto the
stage is a fully rounded character, is not at all inter-
changeable with any other, and is individually portrayed with his own limitations and his own freedom.

There is, however, something else that is also truly
miraculous, and that is the strange beauty of the play.
The horrors of the world are exhibited in their most
extreme form; nothing is glossed over. But the inex-
orability with which the truth is laid bare gives the
tragedy an incandescent quality.

Electra

The Background

Many years have passed since Clytemnestra murdered her husband, Agamemnon, on his return from Troy. She rules over Mycenae with her accomplice, Aegisthus, who is now her husband. Two daughters by her first marriage are still living in the palace. The younger, Chrysothemis, has since made her peace with her mother, but her older sister, Electra, still openly despises Clytemnestra for the crime she committed. Hardly a day passes without her shedding tears for her dead father. Since her hate is so great that it constitutes a danger to her mother and stepfather, she is confined to the maids' quarters and treated like a slave.

Despite this, however, she does not submit. Her strength is sustained by the hope that her brother, Orestes, whom she had spirited away to safety with kinsmen in Phocis after Agamemnon's murder, will return and avenge their father's death. Orestes is now grown up and, since he has repeatedly given her to understand that he will, indeed, come and avenge Agamemnon, she finds it difficult to understand the delay. But the time has now come. Three strangers have arrived in Argos dressed as travelers. They are, in fact, Orestes, the old family servant who had accompanied the child Orestes in his flight from Mycenae, and his close friend, Pylades.

Electra is one of Sophocles' later plays. He was more than eighty years old when he wrote it, and he saw much in a different light. Yet he has not gone so far as the younger Euripides, whose own *Electra*, put on in 413 B.C., perhaps inspired him to write this play. Euripides gave a modern, psychological appraisal of the matricide, as it were; Sophocles uses his new interpretation of the old theme (an interpretation which also differs radically from that of Aeschylus in the *Oresteía*) to develop his own conception of heroic tragedy.

Electra

It is sunrise as three men arrive in front of the palace in Mycenae. They are fully aware of the dangers of their enterprise. Indeed, Orestes has hesitated so long because the dreadful nature of the deed required careful reflection. But now, much against his will, Orestes decides to follow the directions of the Delphic oracle and carry out the act by subterfuge: he is to return to his homeland bearing no arms and heading no army.

It is with great emotion that Orestes, in disguise, now stands in front of the palace and thinks of his father's throne, to which he is the rightful heir. But he is seized by fear: cries of lament issue from the palace. The Old Man urges him on. They must do what they have to do. Of first importance is sanctification of the deed. This can be achieved by performing a ritual sacrifice at Agamemnon's grave. Heeding his admonition, Orestes and the others go to Agamemnon's grave. After this the plan specifies getting the Old Man into the palace so that he can estimate the situation there. The ruse the three have devised is that the Old Man, carrying an urn, will seek an audience with the queen and tell her that Orestes was killed while contending in a chariot race. The urn is supposed to contain his ashes, which the Old Man has brought to the queen so that Orestes' remains can be buried in his native soil.

Scarcely have the three men left than the cries of lament come closer. Electra enters from the left wing of the palace. She is dressed in the black garb of a maid and wears a mask with features expressive of her deep grief. There is music as she gives vent to her incessant sorrow, and this is then followed by antiphony as the Chorus of Mycenean women joins in. They are full of pity for the unhappy Electra and gently try to urge her away from her grief toward a new life.

The Chorus sings that she mourns without measure. But where, Electra asks, is there a measure of misery? If so monstrous a deed remains unavenged, where among men abides a sense of shame and respect? Does she not live in the house that shelters her father's murderers? Does she not see Aegisthus sitting in her father's chair? Does she not know that he sleeps with her vile mother in her father's bed? Is she not shaken to see that the couple live, not in fearful anticipation of the Furies, but in laughter, even giving thanks to the gods? There is only one thing left to her: not to let them forget that Orestes is alive.

Only when Clytemnestra hears of Orestes' coming, does she show fear. And even then she does her best to disguise this fear by her ranting and raving. In such a situation is it any wonder that Electra should so continually mourn and hate?

As if to show the happiness that might have been Electra's had she submitted to her mother and Aegisthus, Chrysothemis now enters dressed in magnificent robes and followed by servants. They are carrying sacrifical offerings. Clytemnestra has been plagued by evil dreams and, in order to rid herself of them, has now commanded that these sacrifices be made at the grave of Agamemnon. She herself dare not appear at his grave. Chrysothemis tries to justify her behavior to her older sister. As she is powerless against the powerful, what sense is there in resisting?

But Electra feels otherwise. She angrily notes that her sister is becoming just like Clytemnestra. As for herself: "Poorly I live, it's true, but at least I honor the dead."

Chrysothemis warns her sister that Clytemnestra and Aegisthus are scheming to imprison her in a far-off cave, where her lamentations will pass unnoticed. This plan is due to be put into effect the moment Aegisthus returns from a journey. Electra welcomes both the news and the fate which lies in store for her. Chrysothemis exhorts her sister "to yield to authority," to be more reasonable. "Father will forgive you," she says. "You may keep silent," replies Electra, "but such is not my way."

Chrysothemis and her train move off. The Chorus does its best to encourage Electra with forecasts of the Justice which must soon surely come. Clytemnestra enters and invokes this same Justice in defense of her crime. She is also carrying sacrificial offerings and is about to pray at the altar of Apollo for deliverance from the evil "night terrors" which plague her. Defending herself to Electra, she attacks Agamemnon: If you had sense you would side with me, not with your depraved father who sacrificed your sister to the gods for Menelaus and Helen.

Electra, however, has her own ideas as to why Clytemnestra killed her husband: "It was succumbing to that evil man with whom you now are living that drew you to it. Had I the power, I myself would seek revenge. But I shall not cease reminding you of Orestes." At this, Clytemnestra furiously calls her daughter "vile and shameless," and she vows that Electra shall pay for her insolence when Aegisthus returns.

While the queen, watched by her daughter, kneels in prayer and makes sacrifices, the Old Man comes out of hiding. He approaches Clytemnestra with "glad tidings": the report that Orestes is dead. With a tremendous wail, Electra breaks down completely. In a long speech notable for its masterly rhetoric, the Old Man dramatically describes Orestes' "fatal" fall from the chariot. Disguised as a mere description of Orestes' death, this speech really serves to glorify the hero, who was famed throughout the whole world. Finally, the Old Man announces that he has come to hand over the urn containing Orestes' remains.

Even Clytemnestra is not unaffected by the news, and the ironic Old Man asks her why this story makes her so dejected. Pulling herself together, and, with noticeable relief in her voice, Clytemnestra says that now at least she will have peace from Electra's threats.

The queen conducts the Old Man into the palace where he may be received in a suitable fashion. For the second time there is antiphony, but it is no longer the old lament, for Orestes, rather than Agamemnon, is now the subject of the mourning. Since the hoped-for avenger is now dead, Electra no longer has anything to live for.

At this point Chrysothemis enters in great excitement. She has found Agamemnon's grave decorated with gifts and with a lock of hair lying on it. Who else can this be but Orestes? Breathless with excitement she throws herself into Electra's arms: "Your day has arrived, now everything will change."

What tragic irony! Electra, deluded into thinking she knows better, tells her sister that Orestes is dead. Now that the immediate impact of the shock has passed, she is able to appraise the situation more objectively. The deed for which she had previously lacked the strength must now be undertaken by the two sisters. Chrysothemis shrinks back in terror, and Electra sees that she will have to go ahead on her own. In her resolution to see the thing through, Electra raises herself to almost superhuman heights. We see and sense her isolation, as the Chorus, recoiling from her, gloomily underlines her tragic greatness.

Electra-Orestes

The recognition scene which follows is constructed with incomparable mastery. Orestes and Pylades enter, followed by men bearing the urn. Quivering with emotion, Orestes hides his anguish at the sight of his sister, worn by all her suffering, and whom he later addresses as "form disgracefully and godlessly abused." He is forced to remain silent as the unhappy girl pours forth her grief in a speech which rises steadily towards an impassioned climax. Wailing her sense of loss in verse after verse, she mourns that the urn holds "all that is left of live Orestes, oh, how differently from what I hoped, do I receive you home."

Once again Electra insists that his death means that she no longer has anything to live for. And as she hammers home the point again and again, Orestes is made to feel how cruel his cunning is, since it makes her unncessarily grieve for his death. He begins to reproach himself for not having acted sooner, as he sees how much his poor sister has had to suffer alone. When Orestes describes her sorrows as *his* sorrows, Electra starts: ". . . you are the only one that ever pitied me." But the brother, who is the only person who can possibly suffer identical sorrows, is still unrecognized by his sister.

So that he may be made fully aware of his tragic deed, Orestes must be shaken out of any complacency stemming from the fact that his decision was one arrived at after consultation with the sacred oracle. The murder he is about to commit should not appear to be carried out simply on divine authority. The human being in Orestes must be aroused so that he will realize that this murder is his own decision, that he must swallow his grief and carry out the deed. Sophocles accordingly puts Orestes in a position in which he finds himself temporarily compelled to turn his back on a sister for whose situation he now sees himself tragically guilty.

But Electra finally recognizes her brother following an arugment during which Orestes has to wrest from her by force the urn which she is tightly clasping. Angered by Electra's obstinacy—she is about to scratch his face to ribbons—Orestes reveals his identity by showing her Agamemnon's signet. Brother and sister embrace in all the rapture of their mutual love.

For a third time there is antiphony. But it is interwoven with dialogue. Electra gradually becomes wilder, more intoxicated, more frenzied, and, worst of all, louder. Orestes, on the other hand, remains calm and opposes her emotional outpourings with firm and sober arguments. As she becomes more emotional, Orestes becomes apprehensive, wishing to separate himself from Electra's outpourings, and begs her to be silent. Coolly and rationally he advises his sister to be careful not to betray his identity by any sign of joy when they are before Clytemnestra. The deed clearly demands a cool head.

Orestes

The noise and excitment have drawn the attention of the Old Man, who comes from the palace and admonishes them. When Electra finally recognizes the old servant, the only one who had remained loyal, she again becomes so excited as to be almost ecstatic. Orestes realizes the need for haste and bids Pylades prepare for action. "We must get inside as quick as ever we can." They enter the palace.

Electra offers up a prayer and then follows them. Just before Clytemnestra's cries ring out, Electra reappears, having been sent out by her brother. Here Sophocles has her give vent to such emotion as to appear almost demented. While the Chorus recoils at the sounds of the woman dying in the palace, Electra drowns these cries with excited shouts exhorting the men to strike yet again.

The great palace gate is opened. Covered in blood and with gory swords in their hands, Orestes and his companions appear within but do not come down the steps. There is a painful silence, and then Electra asks: "Orestes, how have you fared?" In one short phrase pregnant with meaning and spoken slowly and deliberately, Orestes answers: "In the house, all is well, if well Apollo prophesied." There is a sound of weapons, and the Chorus and Electra urge the men to conceal themselves inside the palace, since this must be Aegisthus approaching. Orestes withdraws. Now that he is saddled with the crime of matricide, he is determined to complete the day's work.

The two murder scenes are so symmetrically constructed that the repetition alone is enough to underline the ritual element. Aegisthus has been told of Orestes' "death." In a show of triumph he appears at the head of his bodyguard and asks where the strangers are. Electra answers with considerable irony: "Inside. They have found their hostess very kind." Aegisthus commands that Orestes' corpse be exhibited before the people—he knows nothing of the urn, and assumes that the body was brought in a coffin. Now that Orestes is dead, Aegisthus has no enemies.

A sad procession emerges from the palace. Orestes, Pylades, and the Old Man come down the steps, their swords concealed beneath their cloaks. They are followed by men carrying the bier, on which, unknown to Aegisthus, lies Clytemnestra's body. Aegisthus commands Orestes to uncover the body, but is told to do so himself. (The revelation of Clytemnestra's corpse underlines Orestes' desire to act in defiance of the oracle and confront Aegisthus man to man without resort to cunning.) As Aegisthus recognizes Clytemnestra and realizes who Orestes really is, Electra can contain herself no longer. She urges her brother to strike him down then and there. But Orestes, determined on the completion of his ritual, drives the whimpering man before him into the palace. Aegisthus is to be killed on the very spot where Agamemnon had lost his life. As Orestes makes this clear, Aegisthus prophetically asks: "Must then this house see the past and future sufferings of its sons?"

Orestes realizes the implication of these words, just as the audience does: his tragedy is not yet finished. Indeed the aura of tragedy surrounding Orestes increases considerably in the last scene. Only Electra is exultant.

Electra can be seen as a return to themes dealt with in *Antigone*, but it delves deeper, and it is more complex. The heroine is not a young girl filled with passionate resentment. Instead, a woman's fate, marked by long suffering, takes on heroic proportions in its opposition to intolerable injustice. The flame of resentment is fed by the sheer powerlessness of her situation and her hope for change. Her isolation is not the result of a single deed, but the consequence of a persistence, which has seemed doomed never to be rewarded. The hoped-for revenge comes only after all hope seemed lost.

Antigone knows that she must die. But, by throwing a few handfuls of dust on the corpse of her beloved brother, she goes to her death pure and unstained. Electra's deed would have been matricide. She would have been driven to it by sheer hate—hate born of the terrible evil done. She therefore cannot be allowed to perform this deed. Instead, a "judge" is needed. Orestes does not act because of his hate, but because he has been charged to do so on sacred authority.

Again the dramatist opens up a whole new dimension: the sacred nature of this commission does not release Orestes from the duties imposed upon him by humanity. While the raving Electra is enjoying the triumph of her hate, Orestes, who has taken her place at the center of the drama, is dragged down to the very depths of human despair, before he can finally rise, a changed man, to complete the sacred mission as a tragically human act.

Compared with *Oedipus the King*, *Electra* has a more open form. Instead of a drama neatly rounded off with the logic of the action coinciding exactly with the logic of the structure, we are given a glimpse into the deepest possibilities of human existence. The polis is pushed further into the background. Excluded from the actual drama, it stands outside the action and fades into an abstraction.

Philoctetes

The Background

Philoctetes, one of the first among the Greek heroes, had been of particular service to Heracles, and upon the latter's death had been given his famous bow and poisoned arrows. While sailing with the Greek fleet to Troy, however, Philoctetes was bitten in his foot by a viper. The wound that developed festered so, that its offensive smell and the hero's cries of agony affected the morale of the troops. For this reason, the leaders of the Greek expedition felt compelled to rid themselves of Philoctetes by leaving him to fend for himself on the uninhabited island Lemnos. Here he has lacked for any kind of medical attention which might possibly have brought him relief, and as a castaway he has had to eke out a precarious existence with the help of his famous bow.

Ten years have now passed, and the Greeks are still fighting before Troy. Then an oracle brings about a change of direction: only with the help of Philoctetes and his bow can Troy be overcome. The Greeks resolve to find him and bring him back so that victory may be theirs. Realizing great cunning must be used if they are to accomplish their aim, they entrust the task to the wily Odysseus, who chooses the young Neoptolemus, the son of the dead hero Achilles, as his companion. Since Neoptolemus had joined the Greek army only after the death of his father, there can be no danger that Philoctetes will recognize him.

The Deceit

The very first scene shows two strongly individualistic figures in action. Odysseus and Neoptolemus have discovered Philoctetes' cave (it is built into the rocky background, and has two entrances which can be reached by steps). Philoctetes himself is not there, but will soon return. Odysseus sets the trap: Neoptolemus must pretend that he has left the battlefield at Troy in anger after an argument with the Atridae, and is now returning home with his men. On hearing this, Philoctetes will undoubtedly ask to be taken along, and in this way he—and his bow—can be enticed aboard the ship and brought to Troy. Odysseus himself is to remain in hiding until Neoptolemus and his men have overpowered Philoctetes.

The young prince finally agrees to this plan, though much against his will, for it runs very much counter to his honest and open nature. But he knows no world where people behave differently. Since the longed-for victory at Troy is at stake, any means of attaining it would seem justified. The decision is made and the

orders are given. Though unconvinced that he is acting for the good, Neoptolemus will do his painful
duty as a soldier.

Odysseus goes off and the Chorus enters. It is made
up of armed men under Neoptolemus' command.
They are dedicated to their commander and would
unquestioningly follow his orders. In the first passage
of antiphony (the purely choral takes second place to
the musically dramatic throughout the whole play)
the young man's feelings are reflected in the manifes-
tations of the Chorus. They show their pity for Philoctetes even before he enters the scene, and it is
vastly intensified when he finally makes his entrance.
His approach is signaled by groans of agony. They see
him stumbling and tripping as he staggers towards
them, presenting a lamentable picture of suffering. He
is wrapped in rags, unkempt and haggard, ravaged by
his long years of suffering, a living corpse, as he calls
himself.

This is what has become of the once-shining hero.
His sickness is chronic, a necessary and evil part of
human existence with consequences determined by
others acting in their own interests. Well might we
ask ourselves why this man—condemned to eternal
suffering, repudiated by his fellows and by the gods—
has not taken his life. But Philoctetes cannot die. So
long as he possesses his bow, there is some hope that he
may some day right the wrong that has been done to
him. If he were simply to die, he would be submitting
to a world in which injustice rules. It is heroic to
continue to live and suffer. As a patient sufferer, Philoctetes resembles Electra and the old man Oedipus.
These heroes are not Christian martyrs for whom suffering is a means to grace. Defiance grows out of their

hate and hope. Their very natures exclude any possibility of submission.

The Truth

Neoptolemus passes his first test in the art of cunning with flying colors. But it is precisely this cunning which brings him nearer and nearer to the hero. Compelled to act as if he knows neither the name nor the fate of Philoctetes, he asks him to describe his whole history and thus reveal the injustice done to him. And since everything combines to further the deceit—the unhappy Philoctetes is overcome with joy when he hears Greek spoken, sees people from Greece, and thinks that the son of his revered Achilles is also the enemy of his enemies—young Neoptolemus finds his action more and more insidious. His true nature begins to assert itself and he is more than a little inclined to disobey his orders and rise up against Odysseus and the world he represents.

Philoctetes unconsciously begins to win this basically very honest young man over to another, different world, to his own world. The deep connections between pity and sympathy (in Greek *sympáthein* means "to suffer with") becomes clear, and before our very eyes a friendship develops between the two men. Meanwhile the impatient Odysseus sends a man, disguised as a trader, with news from Troy that the Greeks are on their way to fetch Philoctetes by force. Obviously they must hurry . . .

Philoctetes is suddenly racked by the most terrible pain (again there is antiphony) and arouses still more pity in Neoptolemus and his men. As he sinks into unconsciousness, Philoctetes hands his bow to his new friend for safekeeping. Further antiphony articulates the dialectic situation, as the Chorus whispers that now is the time to act. But Neoptolemus cannot bring himself to make off with the bow, and Philoctetes regains consciousness.

By this time the young man has had enough of lies and subterfuge and, with the bow in his hand, he divulges the whole villainous business, the whole tissue of lies and deceit. We can imagine what a terrible awakening this must be for Philoctetes, who thought that rescue was at hand. Moreover, by taking his bow Neoptolemus robs him of his means of survival; he is a "nothing" without it. Gradually the hero's distress gives way to curses.

Moved by pity, Neoptolemus is about to return the bow to Philoctetes when Odysseus steps out of hiding. Coldly and viciously he commands Neoptolemus' men to seize Philoctetes, who is powerless without his bow. This triumph seemingly assured, Odysseus forces a new turn in events. The gulf between the two worlds —the deceitfully political and the heroically honest— becomes evident in the dialogue that follows. Odysseus himself finally has to realize that this man would be totally intolerable in the Greek camp before Troy because of the sheer power of his accusations. He orders his men to let him go. We have his bow and do not need him. "Come, Neoptolemus. Do not look at him. Your noble-mindedness may spoil all that is at stake."

We must ask ourselves whether Odysseus is nothing but the villain he is usually seen as. Has Sophocles changed his mind so drastically since *Ajax*, in which he portrays Odysseus as the very voice of reason? By no means. Odysseus is still the voice of reason. It is only the poet's opinion of politics that has changed. Odysseus had no personal interest in the marooning of Philoctetes. He did, indeed, have a part in it because of his interest in his country's cause, which would have suffered had Philoctetes remained with the army. Again he uses his cunning simply as a means to an important end: the capture of Troy.

On one occasion Odysseus spells out his stand very clearly. He is always there when something necessary has to be done, and he has always pursued a matter with one thing in mind: its successful conclusion. The end justifies the means, in other words, and what is this other than Realpolitik? Those who reproach him for this view are indirectly condemning the methods of politics in general. Odysseus' views are succinctly stated in the first scene of the play, when he tries to put Neoptolemus' fears to rest:

> I know it is not your natural bent to stray from truth and take a person in. But victory is glorious. Therefore listen to my words. Some other time we shall be honest. Henceforth, I vow that we shall be the most fair-minded of men.

The Turning Point

Still in the shadow of the great Odysseus, young Neoptolemus leaves the scene with him. The Chorus remains behind to watch over Philoctetes while the ship prepares to set sail. A new antiphony brings the most wretched and pathetic hero to raving desperation, and he is almost ready to throw himself off the rocks into the abyss below. Neoptolemus hurries back, followed by Odysseus, who vainly tries to detain him. But the younger man has finally gone over to the side of justice. Secure in the knowledge that it is better to do right than to obey the dictates of expediency, he wishes to return Philoctetes' bow to him.

When Odysseus warns Neoptolemus that the Greeks will prevent him from carrying out this purpose, he is simply and briefly informed that "He who sides with justice has nothing to fear."

Odysseus' reply indicates his uncompromising position: Neoptolemus—and not the Trojans—is now his enemy. They draw swords, but Neoptolemus' men throw themselves between them. Odysseus rushes off to report to the army what has happened, and vows that the younger man shall not escape punishment.

Neoptolemus can match neither the intellectual cunning of Odysseus nor the heroic stature of Philoctetes. We are therefore forced to marvel all the more at his simple decision in favor of decency. Having made amends for his dishonest behavior by restoring the bow, he now attempts, with the same simplicity, to win over Philoctetes, who has called upon the gods to let the Greeks perish with Troy! He tells him that the sorrows which are of his own making are worse than his pain, and that care will be available to him if he returns to Troy. He also points out that the oracle had prophesied that Philoctetes would achieve great fame among Troy's conquerors.

However, the hero rejects such an opportunistic solution. One man's evil behavior and character invariably rubs off on his fellows—as Neoptolemus has just seen. For Philoctetes, the crux of the matter lies just here: if he accedes, will he be giving up his opposition to evil, accepting it as a part of life about which nothing can be done? Only by disassociating himself from this evil, can he remain unsullied by it.

Somewhat discomfitted by this argument, Neoptolemus nevertheless counters by saying that however true this may be, Philoctetes can be relieved of his sufferings only by accompanying him to Troy. But Philoctetes remains adamant and vows never to go back to the Greeks willingly.

An impasse seems to have been reached, and Philoctetes cuts short all further argument by rather forcefully suggesting that Neoptolemus do what he initially promised: take Philoctetes back home. The young man agrees and they set off for the ship as antiphony breaks out.

The situation is seemingly one of stalemate. On the one hand we have Philoctetes adamantly opposed to the world; on the other hand we have the world as it exists, with Odysseus as its prime representative. Only one thing is new. Sophocles has placed Neoptolemus between these two irreconcilables. Born good, Neoptolemus is nevertheless provoked to evil by representatives of the evil world. Pity and good judgment, however, bring out his true character again, and, by returning the bow, he demonstrates that Philoctetes' harsh judgment of the world is not wholly true.

The fact that a human being decides in favor of the right justifies the *deus ex máchina* apparition of Heracles, who orders Philoctetes to go to Troy. Evil does not reign supreme in this world after all; political considerations alone do not determine our experience. The desire and will to do right, to consider morality before expediency and to oppose power whenever it seeks to repress justice, this, too, is a force which moves the world.

The hero who does not submit is able to arouse pity among some, perhaps only a few, of his fellowmen by virtue of his suffering and his greatness. The tragedy of Philoctetes' situation is therefore not entirely hopeless. And the gods accordingly demonstrate that they can be both inimical and, from time to time, well-disposed toward mankind. And so Heracles, the demigod, is able to appear and show Philoctetes the predetermined road to salvation. Heracles' fate was like his: labors and suffering. Overcoming both, he gained immortality. Philoctetes is destined for the same reward.

Today, we see this play differently from the way it was seen by previous generations. We are not put off by Philoctetes' disease—as was Hegel, for example, who thought the play was impossible to produce "because of the stinking ulcers, the groans and shrieks." On the contrary, the disease, together with the injustice done to the sick man despite (or because of) the disease, emphasizes the true picture of the world as it really is. Horror and cruelty have always been a means of jolting the audience out of its accustomed complacency.

And yet the end of this play can never quite achieve the same compelling impact that it must have had on Sophocles' contemporaries. Perhaps some device of the epic theater could come to the aid of the director here and make it possible to focus the audience's attention on the dialectic tension leading up the predetermined conclusion rather than on the actual events. This, surely, would be in accordance with the dramatist's original intentions.

In this way, the audience would no longer be disturbed by the appearance of the *deus ex máchina*, and would not see it as merely a miraculous event. Instead, it would see the end simply as the restatement of a fact, which had already been determined, but which this powerful dramatist had managed to treat in such a way that we almost no longer believe in the eventual fall of Troy.

Oedipus at Colonus

Mythological Background

Many years have passed since Creon refused Oedipus' request to be driven out into the mountains. Instead, Oedipus had been forced to live in the palace as a virtual prisoner while Creon ruled and his two sons were growing up. Gradually he had come to realize, as he thought over his life again and again, that he had gone too far in his expiation. The play gives no information about the events which finally lead up to his expulsion from Thebes. It is, however, hinted that there is a connection between this event and the accession to the throne by his two sons.

Other versions of the myth tell of a quarrel between the father and his sons, during the course of which Oedipus pronounced a curse on them. At all events, Polynices and Eteocles initially ruled jointly over Thebes. Only the two daughters remained true to their father, Antigone guiding her blind father into the mountains, and Ismene later bringing him news from the city. His life is so wretched that he feels death creeping up on him, although he is hardly fifty years old. He remembers the promise that he would finally find repose in Athens, and has now started out for this city with Antigone.

Shortly before the action of the play begins, there has been a coup d'état in Thebes: Eteocles has seized power with Creon's help and has driven his brother out of the country. Polynices has gone to Argos to raise an army and prepare for war against Thebes. But now, once again, an oracle fixes everyone's attention on Oedipus: blessed will be that land where Oedipus finally comes to rest, dead or alive.

This tragedy, written in 406 B.C., was first performed in 401 B.C., five years after Sophocles' death at the age of ninety. He had been unable to have his play produced during his lifetime, because no theatrical performances were given during the siege of Athens by Sparta and Thebes. He dedicated the work to the doomed polis.

Everything about this play conjures up a bygone era. Once again the old tragic theater in all its greatness and beauty is captured. Once again the spirit which Athens represented is called up, not so much Athens as a historical reality as Athens as an idea, as the idea of the polis. Within the historical context of decline, this hymn of praise was of burning actuality. We can, of course, no longer recapture this aspect of the play. We are simply left with the work of art.

This posthumous tragedy harks back to *Oedipus the King*, to the greatest of Sophocles' plays. But how does the deposed blind king get to Athens? A legend widely known in Sophocles' birthplace tells how Oedipus found his last resting place in the sacred grove of the Eumenides at Colonus. This provided the theme. In Aeschylus' last play, Orestes' atonement is achieved through the transformation of the vengeful Erinyes into the kinder and well-disposed Eumenides. In Sophocles' last play, atonement can be achieved only because there is a polis in this world which both fears the Erinyes *and* honors the Eumenides. Where justice counts for more than power, an innocent man struck by the gods can be absolved by man's sound judgment. The oracle is demythologized, as it were.

The play describes how Oedipus approaches death, and how political power tries to seize him in order to secure its own salvation. Such strong beliefs in the effective power of heroes' graves were still current even in enlightened Athens, as is proven by the state decree requiring that the bones of Theseus be brought from Skyros to Athens (468 B.C.). Creon's purpose is solely to see to it that Oedipus is buried in Thebes. This is to be done in the name of the polis and with the knowledge of Eteocles.

Creon therefore attempts to take Oedipus by main force. Such behavior toward a man who is little more than a living corpse is repulsive to us, but Sophocles has Oedipus able to choose where he shall die. Oedipus does not decide in favor of one political power or another but simply in favor of that polis where justice reigns. Considering the political situation at the time the play was conceived and written, Oedipus cannot be seen as a patriotic glorification of Athens by the Athenian poet: the old Athens (or, to put it more precisely, the idea of the polis as it originated in Athens) had developed into what Thebes actually *is* in the play.

Sophocles' choice of Colonus as the scene of the

action was, in part, bitterly ironic, for in 411 B.C. it had witnessed the lamentable spectacle of a wilful repudiation of democracy by the people. By having the sanctification of the dying hero take place mysteriously as Oedipus disappears leaving no trace of a grave, Sophocles indicates to the Athenians the low point to which their nationalism and cult of the hero brought them. The blessing Oedipus bestows upon the city by his decision to remain there and die is connected with the reason that moved him to this choice: he is acting in favor of the polis which ancient Athens once was, or aspired to be.

Oedipus at Colonus is a work of deep and painful beauty. It contains more music than any of the poet's other tragedies. Nature itself plays an eloquent role; there is the sacred grove (just as it actually forms the background to the bare scene in the Theater of Dionysus) and the view over the valleys to the sea. The first and last parts are full of holiness and sanctification. In each case there is a scene which serves as a link to the middle part. These scenes are constructed and positioned in such a way, however, that they are part of the central section, are overlapped by it so to speak. And yet at the same time these connecting links do not prevent the central part from standing out in sharp contrast to the two parts flanking it.

First Part

Nightingales can be heard singing in the grove. An old blind man comes onto the scene, feeling his way with his staff and supporting himself with his other arm round the shoulders of a girl. He presents a wretched picture; his clothers are ragged and filthy, his hair shaggy and matted. Both wear masks indicating dire need and deep distress, and they shuffle in dragging their feet wearily. The old man looks just about exhausted. Their entire belongings and the little food they have been able to beg are carried in a bag.

Is this what has become of Oedipus? And where is the heroic Antigone of the earlier play? They have reached their goal—Athens and the grove of the Eumenides. Oedipus sinks down on the steps leading to the grove, but scarcely has he done so than a terrified passerby admonishes them for trespassing on holy ground. However, the man clearly suspects that this old blind man is no ordinary person, for he straightaway promises to do as asked and call King Theseus. But first he informs the people of Colonus, who quickly arrive in some excitement. They form a Chorus of old men and are soon seized with dread (expressed musically and dramatically) when they learn of the identity of the accursed man who has desecrated the holy place: "Away with you! Out with you! Leave our land!" But Antigone movingly wins the Chorus over and manages to change its shudder of fear into one of pity, as it is confronted with the spectacle of Oedipus radiating holiness.

At this point Sophocles inserts the connecting scene. Ismene, accompanied by a servant, comes riding in on a mule. She is dressed in wanderer's garb. Falling into her father's arms, she reports on events in Thebes and announces that the new oracle has decreed that a successful outcome of the war depends upon Oedipus' being buried near Thebes. Creon knows Oedipus' whereabouts and is coming to seize him. On hearing this, the Chorus hesitates no longer, and accedes readily to Oedipus' request—to the suppliant's plea for protection.

In return, however, Oedipus must leave the steps at the entrance to the sacred grove and take up a position outside the forbidden area. Here he rests until the beginning of the third part, after agreeing to the purification ritual which concludes the first part. As Ismene takes his place in the actual cleansing, Oedipus is, according to custom, once again confronted with the horrible stain on his life, with his patricide and incest, with a sin which, as he solemnly protests, was committed in all innocence.

The Central Part

Theseus arrives on the scene. He is an ideal figure, shining with the divine light of the polis ideal he represents, and the very embodiment of the highest ideals of the political become one with the human. Oedipus promises him the blessing which the oracle has assigned as his to bestow. In return Theseus not only offers him the protection due to him as a suppliant, but also confers upon him the citizenship of the state. After entrusting Oedipus to the care and protection of the people of Colonus he retires to the beach, where he is to continue sacrificing to Colonus' patron god.

Almost immediately, Creon approaches from the other side at the head of Theban troops. Hypocritically and cynically, he "invites" Oedipus to return to the people of Thebes. But the blind man knows from Ismene why Creon extends this offer. Looking around, Creon discovers Ismene in the grove, and he has her seized by his men. He also commands that Antigone

be taken, since he well knows how he can best bend
Oedipus to his will. The girls are led off. As the
Chorus shrinks back in alarm before Creon's drawn
sword, Theseus enters with armed men.

On hearing what has happened, he orders his men to
intercept the Theban troops as they flee with Antigone and Ismene. He presents Creon with an ultima-
tum, which the hypocritical Theban answers by saying that he had never expected a just state like Athens
to accord asylum to a parricide who has ravished his
mother. Theseus now delivers an apologia, with which
the Chorus fully concurs. "This man has expiated his
guilt." The scene ends with Creon being taken hostage
as they all leave to join the troops who are to intercept
the Thebans and free the girls.

The choral song which follows portrays imaginary
battles and glorious victories, and then Ismene and
Antigone enter and rush into their father's arms.
Theseus follows. He waves away Oedipus' thanks and
announces that a stranger has arrived from Argos seeking protection and wishing to speak to Oedipus. The
latter flares up in a sudden rage at this news: obviously
it must be Polynices, who will now try to achieve
what his foe Creon has just failed to do. Only after
remonstrations from Theseus and Antigone does Oedipus reluctantly allow Theseus to fetch the stranger.

The struggle for Oedipus' living corpse comes to an
end with the Polynices scene which now follows. This
scene serves as a link to the last part, just as the Ismene
scene had been a link to the central part. Three times
Polynices tries to break Oedipus' stubborn silence. But
his request for forgiveness is of no avail, neither is his
reference to the injustice done him by his brother,
which he now uses in self-justification.

When Polynices drives home to him that both father and son are here in the same boat—beggars and
exiles—the sick, old man flies into a terrible rage, a
rage which is the cause of his death and which thereby
opens the way for his sanctification. How could this
villainous son, who planned to kill his own father, possibly put himself on the same level as one whose sufferings and afflictions were tragic because he could not
be blamed for actions committed in all innocence?
How could he possibly talk of an inherited curse? No
curse is inherited, for how, otherwise, could his
daughters be so different from his infamous sons? The
reason for Polynices' plight is that he has disregarded
the old unwritten laws. (We will remember that in
the earlier tragedy Antigone had also invoked these
old laws).

Suddenly the dying man takes on an aura of holiness
and breaks out with a prophetic curse:

> You most evil of all. Away with you. I have cast
> you out. From now on you have no father. And
> let this curse go with you. The soil of your father-
> land shall become your Hades. You shall fall by
> your brother's hand while killing him. Now go
> and tell the people of Thebes why Oedipus
> offers such gifts to his sons.

We cannot rationally explain the poetic greatness of
these lines. They are a mixture of Old Testament
wrath and the ecstasy of a prophet through whom a
god is speaking. From the psychic wound of which
the wretched, unwitting, and worthless son reminds
his father, once more streams Oedipus' lifelong agony
and all the pathos connected with it. It precipitates the

death by which he is cleansed. His sufferings end with his life, and the demon leaves him. Now he can call Theseus and take his last steps on this earth. The central part ends with Polynices' farewell; he goes off knowing that there is no turning back for him and that he must live out his accursed life to its end.

The Last Part

In his cursing of his sons bleeds Oedipus' wounded love. He speaks to his daughters of his great love for them. His last words are directed at the sun, whose warmth and light he shall no longer feel: "O light not shining for me. Once you were mine. Now this is the last I will feel of you."

Oedipus does not easily take leave of this earthly life. But a miracle takes place: without any help at all, the frail, old man arises, and blind though he is, actually leads Theseus to the place where he must die. Fully upright, he strides down the steps to the grove, followed by the girls. There is thunder and lightning, though the evening sky is clear. The Chorus is overwhelmed with awe. There is music and song.

A messenger emerges from the grove to report what has happened. When Oedipus had bidden his daughters farewell, a voice cried out: "Oedipus! Oedipus! Why do you delay? Too long do you tarry." It was the messenger of death. What happened then, and how and where Oedipus disappeared, only Theseus could have seen, and there is no trace of a grave. The sisters are looking in vain for it, so that they can pay their last respects to their father. Their future will be untold suffering now that he is gone, and their old sorrow will seem so much sweetness in comparison with what is to come.

In the midst of the general lamentation, Theseus tells the sisters that he cannot allow them near the spot where Oedipus had disappeared. Oedipus promised him that Athens should be safe from its enemies so long as no one trod upon the earth he last stood upon.

The blessing of the unknown grave will, from this moment, begin to take effect. But what remains for the girls to do? They will go to Thebes and try to prevent their brothers from killing each other. But we know what is in store for them.

We are left to reflect on the nature of death. Life seems to end gently enough in music, and it is then in death that we find mercy. In this drama of redemption, we find a choral song whose words have as much meaning to us today as they could ever have had. Not to be born is superior to all wisdom. But once having come into this world, surely the second best is to go quickly whence you came. For once you have imprudent youth behind you, what pain is there that may not strike you? At last devoid of power and companionship, we succumb to old age, wherein all bitter things abide.

So sang the chorus.

SOPHOCLES ON THE CONTEMPORARY STAGE

Women of Trachis
NEW SCHOOL FOR SOCIAL RESEARCH

A number of Broadway actors, some of them busy in current plays, have helped a series of Sunday night dramatic readings at the New School for Social Research get off to a fine start. Eli Wallach, Anne Jackson, Maureen Stapleton, Alfred Ryder and James Dean, to name the outstanding ones, were among those performing in the past weekend's program, which, in advance, sounded like a formidable highbrow affair—a double-bill of Euripides' *Electra* and Sophocles' *Trachiniae*, the latter in an Ezra Pound version. But it turned out to be a stimulating, enjoyable evening thanks chiefly to the uninhibited Mr. Pound and actors who served him well.

His *Women of Trachis* is no respectful translation but a startling, free-swinging adaptation, often slangy, which raises solid laughs and also gets across the original's painful, harrowing climax. And even here, in the midst of Herakles' prolonged dying scene, there are comedy moments, for the strangely brilliant Mr. Pound not only switches from stark drama to humor without pausing but packages them sometimes in the same phrase . . .

Though *Women of Trachis* arouses easy laughs with anachronisms like "pip-squeak . . . had a letch for the girl . . . screwball. . . . etc.," it is no slangy vulgarization of Sophocles but a curiously harmonious blending of modern humor and old tragedy. Like T. S. Eliot in this, though the two men otherwise are entirely different, Mr. Pound shuttles without advance notice from the sublime to the comically trivial, and vice versa, a tendency that is apparently encouraged by our uneasy times.

Louis Sheaffer, *Brooklyn Daily Eagle*, Feb. 17, 1954.

Antigone
THÉÂTRE NATIONAL POPULAIRE
JEAN VILAR, DIRECTOR

Clarity of speech and simplicity of interpretation are the keynote of Mr. Vilar's latest production of Sophocles's *Antigone*, his first essay in classical drama, if one omits the Gide version of *Oedipus*. "Est-ce que je parle clair et net?" asks the Soldier of Creon (in André Bonnard's translation) with a bluntness that borders on insolence. Every one of the characters expresses himself or herself in just such terms. As a result, the moral conflict is shorn of all fortuitous excrescence and bluntly driven home as never before. Whether this is the right, or the ideal way of projecting an ancient theatrical convention to a modern audience in Avignon, consisting for the greater part of young people, who are seeing Sophocles for the first time, is an academic debating point. That it succeeds here, and succeeds mightily well, is plain for everyone to see.

The Times (London), July 25, 1960.

Electra
THE GREEK THEATER ASSOCIATION
DIMITRIOS RONDIRIS, DIRECTOR

So swift and believable is the personal drama of Electra's overweening hatred that the presence of the chorus, admirably constituted though it is, occasionally distracts the spectator. Here is a case of trouble rising out of dramatic virtue, for the chorus does its job effectively in classical tradition, while [Aspassia] Papathanassiou and her fellow players are succeeding so well in their own work, which is less stylized, more susceptible of contemporary understanding than the often partisan, sometimes prophetic and sometimes fallible chorus.

Take the scene in which Electra first hears of the supposed death of Orestes. Her grief is concentrated in a single cry. Nothing more is needed. The posturing of the chorus in its multiple grief is superfluous, almost ridiculous.

This chorus is a highly editorial group, too. It is often said that Sophocles does not pass judgment on the characters in his *Electra*, but the chorus certainly does, taking up accusatory poses when Electra berates Clytemnestra, recoiling in horror when Clytemnestra damns her daughter in return.

There is no need to dwell too long, though, on classical conventions that seem strange to us, three thousand years after Sophocles wrote. He was in the avant garde when there was hardly any garde, and the real wonder of this performance is that so much of the play retains our interest, even though it may not arouse our passions.

Joseph Morgenstern, *New York Herald Tribune*, Sept. 20, 1961.

Philoctetes
GROUP OF ANCIENT DRAMA
ANTHONY KELLER

How do you produce a play for which there is no living tradition of performance in English? It is a hard question; in the case of Greek drama there seem essentially to be two answers. Either you try for the sort of massive, stately, stylized, ritualistic performance that the plays received, according to such records as remain to us, at the Festivals of Dionysus in ancient Athens; or you stage your play more or less realistically, and try to make it intelligible to modern audiences by approximating modern theatrical conventions.

The outdoor East River Park Amphitheatre with its huge two-level acting area and its steeply-banked, curving rows of benches with room for 2000 spectators, is well-suited to a classically-oriented production. The play, on the other hand, is built on a very neatly poised and poignantly modern dilemma: We need Philoctetes and his magic bow in order to conquer Troy; do we kidnap him and take the bow, or allow him the right of self-determination and take the chance of losing the war? With its instantly comprehensible motivations, its myth suffused by realpolitik, *Philoctetes* is perhaps better suited than any other surviving Greek play for a modern, realistically detailed production.

The Group of Ancient Drama's effort inclined tentatively sometimes in one direction, sometimes in the other, sometimes in both simultaneously, and as a result was equally deficient in classical magnificence and in modern subtlety. . . .

Julius Novick, *Village Voice*, Aug. 8, 1964.

Electra
NEW YORK SHAKESPEARE FESTIVAL
GERALD FREEDMAN, DIRECTOR

What is most out of order in this production is simply the lack of a common language among the performers—and by language I also mean gesture, manners, that particular, unbidden something which reveals a sense of time and place. It is analogous but not identical to "the hum" Lionel Trilling speaks of in referring to that quality of everyday life absent in literature of all periods except one's own. The Zeitgeist is closer to what I mean but not quite it. I've chosen to call it the communal persona, that common bearing by which the world perceives us. This communal persona is what makes an Odets production by American actors seem so absolutely right. The presence of the persona can make *Electra* heartrending to us for the participants who then tear at one another are in fact devouring nothing less than pieces of themselves. The sense of the common life is what makes a civil war so harrowing. It is what makes the hatred between people who have formerly loved one another so especially bitter.

Arthur Sainer, *Village Voice*, Aug. 12, 1964.

Antigone
LIVING THEATRE (IN PARMA, ITALY)
JUDITH MALINA, DIRECTOR

Creon walked between the flower of his city's youth, placed a hand casually between the young men's legs, and ripped upwards. The young men fell to the ground screaming. Castrated, they could now be sent off to fight Argos, and Creon thrust them off the stage into the aisles, where they became possessed fighters, slashing away at the enemy like maniacs, inches from our faces. The war exploded into the auditorium, Eteocles and Polyneikes were killed, their bodies laid on stage. The actors climbed back again, Judith Malina stepped forward as Antigone to speak (in Italian) the first lines of Brecht's narrative verses introducing each scene (played in English), and after 20 minutes of cries, moans, screams and gasps, the text had begun.

This remarkable opening paves the way for a production which succeeds in making Sophocles more immediate than any English language performance I have ever seen. What the Living Theatre have done is to draw on their affinity with Artaud to materialize in sharp physical gestures the imagery and values which run through the play. A character speaks of dogs and vultures defiling Polyneike's corpse, and the actors momentarily become those dogs. Antigone attacks the elders for being craven . . . and the citizens become a shaking spineless mass. . . .

Michael Kustow, *The Times* (London),
April 8, 1967.

Oedipus Rex
STRATFORD FESTIVAL IN ONTARIO (ON FILM)
TYRONE GUTHRIE, DIRECTOR

Most movies are supposed to enlarge on a play, to take it beyond the narrow limits of a stage. *Oedipus Rex* does not, and this is its special genius. The film is true to the conventions of Greek drama. It has classical purity that is stunning.

All the actors wear grotesque masks. In Athenian times this enabled spectators to identify the characters far below. In the movie these masks are not strictly necessary, but they still have great symbolic value. They are also very striking in design.

Oedipus has a huge mask and crown of kingly gold. The blind seer Tiresias is a smooth white skull with a beaked nose and two gaping black holes for eyes. Obviously such a man will make no happy prophecies. The facile Creon is a greenish bronze mask with quizzical eyebrows and a shifty look. The lady Jocasta is a silver face etched in sorrow, and the suppliants of the chorus are drab and plebian. . . .

This *Oedipus Rex* is as stylized as an Oriental dance, and to some moviegoers this will be a serious flaw. For the masked and ritualistic actors don't seem to be human beings, but legendary figures somewhere be-

tween man and god. They may fascinate us, but they
do not touch us deeply.

And yet this is also the film's greatest distinction.
For though it ignores the rules of moviemaking in the
twentieth century, it has very much in common with
the production that celebrated the spring festival of
430 B.C. in the theater of Dionysius, on the slopes of
the Acropolis.

William K. Zinsser, *New York Herald Tribune*,
Jan. 8, 1957.

Antigone
REPERTORY THEATER OF LINCOLN CENTER
JOHN HIRSCH, DIRECTOR

That the *Antigone* of Sophocles is a great imperish-
able play is happily in no serious doubt. Such doubt as
it might be in was put very much to the test last night
by its execrable staging by the Lincoln Center Repertory Company at the Vivian Beaumont Theater. The
scenery was splendid: The production's basic and ir-
remediable fault came when they brought on the actors. . . .

The pattern of the play has that sharp simplicity so
favored by Sophocles, where action and outcome are
the hammer and anvil of the drama. Given these characters and these circumstances there is never any
doubt about the outcome. They are a mirror for our
sins, a lesson for our tragedies. You can learn humanity from Shakespeare or Euripides or Aeschylus. From
Sophocles you can only learn the facts of death.

The English version is by Dudley Fitts and Robert
Fitzgerald. Although doubtless it aspires to poetry, it

is unfortunately prose of the very kind that made the adjective prosaic the word it is today.

Clive Barnes, *The New York Times*, May 14, 1971.

Antigone
REPERTORY THEATER OF LINCOLN CENTER
JOHN HIRSCH, DIRECTOR

Reflecting the tone of the Fitts-Fitzgerald version, the twin aims of John Hirsch's staging appear to be clarity and freshness. These aims have been notably achieved. The text is spoken naturally yet with eloquence; rather than declamation, there is an intense concern for the verbal beauties of the dialogue. The approach deepens the tragedy's impact and enhances its immediacy. The series of confrontations—between the principal characters, between Creon and Teiresias, or between Creon and the chorus (impressively led by Charles Cioffi and Pauline Flanagan)—acquire a kind of concentration without diminishing the awesome fatefulness of the Sophoclean plot.

Since *Antigone* is a play for all ages, the inevitable temptation for those reviving it must be to single out for particular emphasis the issues it touches which are uppermost at any given moment. Certainly the immemorial conflict between the state's supremacy, as symbolized by Creon, and Antigone's individual freedom appealing to a higher law is as relevant today as it was 2,400 years ago. So is the clash between youth and age. Mr. Hirsch has let the relevancies fall where they may, without giving them undue emphasis. Except for the soldier's visored helmets, he has not introduced the artifice of masks—in itself, of course, a more naturalistic way of presenting the characters.

John Beaufort, *The Christian Science Monitor*,
May 14, 1971.

Antigone
REPERTORY THEATER OF LINCOLN CENTER
JOHN HIRSCH, DIRECTOR

Perhaps it's an accident of the times or an irony hurled down by the gods, but the John Hirsch production of Sophocles's *Antigone* . . . resonates with so much contemporary social relevance one feels batted back and forth between antiquity and today's headlines. This makes it difficult to find the elemental bleakness of classical Greek tragedy. The irony is that the English version by Dudley Fitts and Robert Fitzgerald was written about fifteen years ago—long before it became modish to talk of Women's Lib, the generation gap, the arrogance of power, a "senseless" foreign conflict or upheaval in the courts. And these very issues, curiously, leap to one's consciousness as the elegiac lines of the ancient tragedy are intoned.

S. K. Oberbeck, *Newsweek*, May 24, 1971.

Oedipus at Colonus
EQUITY LIBRARY THEATER
DAVID BAMBERGER, DIRECTOR

Blanche Du Bois wasn't the only one who ultimately depended on the kindness of strangers. So, it seems, did Oedipus.

And what finally happened to him? According to *Oedipus at Colonus*, which the Equity Library has bravely staged at its uptown Masters Theater, the worn-out old exile found refuge with King Theseus and the Athenians. Resisting ploys by his son and by an old enemy to lure him back home, he succumbs with his two daughters at his side. The old king marches off stage for a quick act of heavenly evaporation.

The Equity people, by a small miracle called intelligence, have done a corking good job with Sophocles's last tragedy, written when he was over 80 and seldom performed in this country. There is very little action. It is the lyrical and poetical beauty of language that counts here.

Howard Thompson, *The New York Times*,
Feb. 14, 1972.

BIBLIOGRAPHY

Adams, S. M. *Sophocles, the Playwright*. Toronto, 1957.

Arnott, Peter. *Greek Scenic Conventions*. Oxford, 1962.

Bates, William N. *Sophocles, Poet and Dramatist*. Reprint, New York, 1969.

Bieber, Margaret. *The Greek and Roman Theatre*. Princeton, N.J., 1961.

Bowra, C. M. *Sophoclean Tragedy*. 2nd ed., Oxford, 1947.

Cameron, A. *The Identity of Oedipus the King: Five Essays on "Oedipus Tyrannus."* New York, 1965.

Cook, A. S., ed. *Oedipus Rex: A Mirror for Greek Drama*. Belmont, Calif., 1963.

Earp, F. R. *The Style of Sophocles*. Cambridge, England, 1944.

Ehrenberg, V. *Sophocles and Pericles*. Oxford, 1954.

Hadas, Moses. *History of Greek Literature*. New York, 1950.

Jackson, John. *Marginalia Scaenica*. New York, 1955.

Kamerbeek, J. C. *The Plays of Sophocles: The Ajax*. Leiden, 1953.

Kitto, H. D. F. *Greek Tragedy*. New York, 1950.

Knox, B. M. W. *The Heroic Temper: Studies in Sophoclean Tragedy*. Berkeley, Calif., 1964.

Lattimore, Richmond. *The Poetry of Greek Tragedy*. Baltimore, Md., 1958.

Long, A. A. *Language and Thought in Sophocles*. New York, 1968.

Murray, Gilbert. *A History of Ancient Greek Literature*. Reprint. New York, 1966.

Opstelten, J. C. *Sophocles and Greek Pessimism*. Trans. by J. A. Ross. Amsterdam, 1952.

Pickard-Cambridge, A. W. *The Theatre of Dionysus in Athens*. Oxford, 1946.

Preller, J. *Griechische Mythologie*. 4th ed. revised by C. Robert. 2 vols. Berlin, 1894–1926.

Shackford, M. H. *Shakespeare, Sophocles: Dramatic Themes and Modes*. New Haven, Conn., 1960.

Webster, T. B. L. *Greek Theatre Production*. London, 1956.

———. *An Introduction to Sophocles*. London, 1969.

Whitman, C. H. *Sophocles: A Study of Heroic Humanism*. Cambridge, Mass., 1951.

Wilamowitz-Moellendorff, T. von. *Die dramatische Technik des Sophokles*. Berlin, 1917.

INDEX